A RAW PERSPECTIVE

PLASTIC REDEMPTION

Turning Trash into Products

By

Innocent Karikoga

Published by

autonomy books

ISBN: 978-1-997657-00-2

Plastic Redemption

Introduction...5

The Plastic Illusion...................................9

A System Built to Fail........................... 28

When Solutions Become Threats................. 42

The Recycling Myth Machine........................ 65

A Simple Solution That Works.....................102

What Is Upcycling?.................................126

Plastic as Currency............................. 152

Products That Prove the Point.................. 167

Why Recycling Failed and Upcycling Works..
191

Last Word.. 203

Introduction

There's a strange kind of silence that falls over a neighbourhood when the garbage truck pulls away. It's a brief, satisfied stillness — the kind that follows a job done, even if poorly. Bins are wheeled back into driveways, people return to their routines, and no one questions where any of it went. Poof. Vanished. One more week of consumption quietly erased. It's modern-day magic: a system designed to help us forget.

But I don't forget.

I was born and raised in Zimbabwe, where waste wasn't just something you could toss on the curb and expect someone else to deal with. We saw our waste. We lived with it. We worked around it. And when we didn't, it worked its way back into our lives — through water, through land, through health.

When I moved to Canada nearly twenty years ago, I thought I had landed in a country that had it figured out. Streets were clean. Garbage was scheduled. Recycling bins were colour-coded and had instructions printed right on the lid. It all felt so efficient, so civilized.

Then I started asking questions.

Where does the recycling actually go? Who sorts it? Who pays for it? What happens when it's contaminated? Why do I keep seeing news articles about Canadian waste turning up in Southeast Asia?

That was when the magic trick began to unravel.

As it turns out, only about 16% of plastic in Canada actually gets recycled. Sixteen. The rest is burned, buried, or dumped. The blue bins aren't a solution — they're a placebo. A guilt-suppressing ritual. We tell ourselves we're helping. We aren't. We're just buying time.

At some point, I stopped being curious and started being angry. The kind of anger that comes from watching smart people do stupid things for just long enough to convince themselves it's normal. I've studied physics. I've studied medicine. I've spent my academic life trying to understand systems — physical, biological, theoretical, logistical. And I can tell you: this isn't a broken system. It's a rigged one. Broken implies it was designed to work. This one never stood a chance.

The government's answer? Form a task force. Roll out a new policy. Assign producers some "responsibility," which really just means they get to outsource the problem for a bit longer while ticking the "action taken" box. By some time in the near future, we're told, producers will be responsible for their packaging waste. Which sounds like a long-winded way of saying, "We'll get back to you in a few years."

The truth is, we already know what works. We just don't want to do it.

I wasn't planning to get involved. This wasn't supposed to be my battle. I was working as a medical writer, consulting on weight management, and spending most of my time helping people solve problems they didn't think had solutions. But something about this issue — the sheer scale of waste, the laziness of the response, the fake solutions — it pushed me past the point of mild discomfort. I stopped waiting for someone to fix it.

I built something myself.

This book is about that decision. It's about taking a problem that's been passed around like a hot potato — from government to corporations to nonprofits and back again — and deciding to hold onto it long enough to do something real.

It's not another "vision for the future" or eco-tech fantasy that needs a hundred million dollars in venture capital. It's practical. Scalable. Deployable tomorrow. And that's precisely what makes it dangerous — because it threatens to do what the current system fears most: succeed without permission.

This book is my attempt to drag the conversation back to reality. To cut through the noise. To show how we got here, why the existing plans won't work fast enough, and what we can do about it — not in theory, but in practice.

There's no hero here. Just trash. Mountains of it. And the quiet, stubborn belief that maybe — just maybe — someone should stop pretending this is normal.

If that sounds like a rebellion, good. Let's begin.

The Plastic Illusion

The Promise of the Blue Bin

It starts with a symbol — three little arrows chasing each other in a triangle, looping endlessly like a promise no one intends to keep. You've seen it a thousand times: stamped onto water bottles, clinging to greasy takeout containers, embossed on the back of snack wrappers. It's our modern secular rosary — the Möbius strip of environmental absolution. It whispers to you every time:

"It's okay. I'm recyclable. You've done your part."

You drop it in the blue bin and walk away a little lighter, convinced your single-use purchase now has a second life. In your mind, a humming factory is waiting — heroic machines melting your coffee cup into a park bench, or maybe a fleece jacket for some grateful child in need. Cue the violins and sunbeams.

But that movie in your head? Total fiction. Most plastic doesn't get recycled. It gets shipped, buried, burned — or worse, becomes someone else's problem.

In Canada, only 9% to 16% of plastic ever sees a second life through recycling. And even that number wobbles depending on how "recycling" is defined. (Is burning plastic for energy really "recycling"? Depends on which industry lobbyist you ask.)

The other 84% to 91%?

- **Landfilled:** entombed in places like Toronto's Green Lane landfill, where microplastics are already being detected in leachate.

- **Incinerated:** "energy recovery" facilities that emit dioxins, CO_2, and a cocktail of toxins — all considered *within regulation*, of course.

- **Exported:** For decades, Canada shipped its recyclables abroad — mostly to countries like China, Malaysia, Indonesia, and the Philippines.

And that's where the illusion truly breaks.

In 2013, Canada sent 103 shipping containers of waste to the Philippines, falsely labelled as recyclable plastics. What was inside? Household garbage. Used diapers. Rotting food. It sat in their ports for years as relations soured. Eventually, in 2019, Philippine President Rodrigo Duterte threatened war if Canada didn't take its trash back.

"Prepare a grand reception. Eat it if you want to," he said. Only then, under international shame, did we retrieve our mess.

But that wasn't a one-off. After China's 2018 ban on foreign plastic waste through its *National Sword* policy, countries like Canada scrambled to find new dumping grounds. Shipments were rerouted to Malaysia and Indonesia, overwhelming local systems. In 2020, Malaysia returned 150 shipping containers of contaminated waste, including dozens from Canada, stating:

"We just want to send a message that Malaysia is not the garbage dump of the world."

Yet here we are, still filling blue bins every week as though the system is working — as though someone, somewhere, is making a Lego set out of your margarine tub.

Here's the dirty secret: most of what goes into that bin was **never recyclable to begin with.**

- Black plastics? Can't be read by optical scanners.

- Coffee cups? Lined with polyethylene — unrecyclable in most facilities.

- Mixed-material wrappers, clamshell containers, pizza boxes with cheese residue? All contaminating the stream.

- Anything with food scraps? Instantly downgraded. Even the "numbered" system of plastic types is mostly performative — codes designed by industry, not governments, with many items being technically recyclable *in theory* but not *in practice.*

So what happens to all this stuff?

Enter the **Recycling Rube Goldberg Machine**.

Municipalities collect your waste. They try to sort it — underfunded, overburdened, sometimes still by hand. Then they bale it into dense cubes and sell it as commodities. If prices are high, and the materials are clean? A win. If not? The bales sit. Or worse — get dumped. Ontario municipalities have quietly landfilled entire loads of "recyclables" when contamination is too high or markets are too weak.

It's not a system. It's theatre. A performance of environmentalism to soothe consumers and protect industry.

And the star of the show? You — the earnest recycler.

You rinse your peanut butter jar. You sort your bins like a surgeon. You believe the triangle. And in return, you get a moral gold star while plastic production soars higher than ever. Why wouldn't it? Plastic is cheap to make, durable, and profitable. Recycling is expensive, messy, and largely unregulated. There is no financial incentive for producers to stop producing waste, especially when they can convince you that you're the one responsible for it.

The ultimate bait-and-switch: consumers shoulder the guilt, corporations pocket the profit.

Meanwhile, industry lobbies peddle "solutions" — biodegradable cutlery that doesn't biodegrade, "compostable" plastics that need industrial facilities that don't exist, carbon offsets that function more like indulgences than impact. All designed to delay real action and give the illusion of progress.

Plastic production is projected to double by 2050, driven by oil companies repositioning themselves for a world that's moving away from gasoline. Petrochemicals are their Plan B, and plastic is the flagship.

And you? You're just trying to figure out whether that greasy sushi tray is recyclable.

Let's be clear: this isn't your failure. It's a systemic betrayal. We were promised that recycling would fix the problem. That with a little sorting, some stickers, and goodwill, we could close the loop.

But loops don't close themselves. And this one was never built to.

Where Does It Really Go?

Let's pretend you're a plastic bottle. Not the kind nestled in a curated Instagram shot of beach cleanups and smiling volunteers, but a regular, boring bottle — say, a Sprite. You had your 15 minutes of fame in someone's sweaty hand, got tossed in a public blue bin, and now — the dream begins.

Except it doesn't.

Your first stop is a **Material Recovery Facility** (MRF), where the magic of "sorting" happens. You're dumped onto a conveyor belt with a thousand of your closest relatives — milk jugs, ketchup bottles, rogue toothpaste tubes — and begin the gauntlet. Human workers (often underpaid, frequently injured) pick through the mess, trying to grab contaminants before machines take over. Infrared scanners try to read what kind of plastic you are. Air jets blow you into different chutes. Magnets yank out metals. It's a symphony of machinery that hums with promise — and fails, spectacularly, when the plastic isn't clean or properly sorted.

See, you might be PET plastic (#1), which has actual value. But if you've got a label that's glued on with a non-water-soluble adhesive, or worse — you're shrink-wrapped in a film with metallic ink — you're now "contaminated." You're not a resource. You're a liability.

If the contamination rate for the load you're in is too high (often above 10% is the death zone), the whole batch could be landfilled. That's right. Tossed in with banana peels and broken dreams.

This isn't a rare outcome. In Calgary, a 2019 audit found that only 33% of what residents put in their blue bins was actually recycled. The rest? Landfill. Toronto estimates that up to 30% of blue bin contents are contaminated and unfit for recycling. In some cities, the number's even worse.

And what about when plastic does get sorted and baled?

That's where it goes *somewhere else*. In theory, it gets sold to a local recycler. In practice, it often enters a global game of hot potato, passed from broker to broker until it lands in a country with lax regulations and cheap labour. Before China's 2018 National Sword policy, Canada shipped over 1 billion kilograms of plastic and paper waste to China every year. When that door slammed shut, the waste started flooding into Vietnam, Thailand, and Malaysia, where informal recyclers burned or dumped what they couldn't use.

In 2019, Malaysian villagers found Canadian plastic trash — including wrappers from Tim Hortons and Sobeys — dumped and torched in open fields. A Greenpeace investigation uncovered dozens of illegal recycling facilities operating without oversight, spewing dioxins and leaving mountains of unprocessable waste behind. The message was clear: our "recyclables" weren't being recycled — they were being outsourced.

Out of sight, out of statistics.

And while the public image of recycling is tidy and circular, the real story is winding and polluted.

Let's follow that Sprite bottle again.

If you're lucky, and pure PET, and the market is stable, you might end up at a domestic recycler. Your body will be shredded, washed (if the plant has proper infrastructure), melted into pellets, and sold to manufacturers to become... another plastic bottle. Maybe.
But you'll probably be downcycled into carpet fibres or construction materials — one last gasp before landfill.

If you're unlucky, you'll be bundled with other "mixed plastic" and shipped abroad, where parts of you might be recycled — and the rest dumped. Or you'll end up in a domestic incinerator labelled "energy recovery," where you'll be burned for heat, emitting CO_2 and leaving behind toxic ash.

You never become a jacket for a child. You become soot in someone's lungs.

And if you're like most plastic, you'll never even make it to a MRF. You'll miss the bin. Or you'll be one of the items not accepted (like black plastic, Styrofoam, or film) and go straight to the landfill. Or — if the wind catches you just right — you'll blow out of a bin, dance across the street, roll into a storm drain, and begin your journey into the ocean.

There are now an estimated 170 trillion plastic particles floating in our seas — and that's just the stuff we can measure. Microplastics have been found in fish, salt, beer, tap water, the clouds, and — just to round out the horror — human blood and placentas. We have embedded plastic into the planet's geology, creating a new fossil layer scientists now call the Plastisphere. Or as the late comedian George Carlin once simply put it, "The earth plus plastic."

And yet we still cling to the myth of the blue bin — this soothing domestic ritual that convinces us we're "part of the solution."

The reality? We're caught in a loop of wishcycling, performative collection, and exported guilt. The system isn't broken. It's doing exactly what it was designed to do: look like a solution without disrupting the source of the problem.

And the source?

That comes next.

The Plastic Machine: Who's Really Making It All?

Let's clear something up right now: You are not the problem.

You didn't ask for everything you touch to be shrink-wrapped in plastic, double-sealed, triple-packaged, and stickered with false promises of recyclability. You didn't choose a society where cucumbers need condoms and avocados come in coffins. That choice was made for you — by the Machine.

Let's name it.

The plastic industry isn't some accidental by-product of modern life. It is a meticulously engineered, massively subsidized, oil-fuelled juggernaut designed to maximize profit and offload responsibility.

At the heart of this machine are the petrochemical companies. **ExxonMobil. Dow. Shell. Chevron Phillips.** The names are familiar, and that's not a coincidence — most of the biggest plastic producers are the same folks cooking the climate. Fossil fuels aren't just burned; they're baked into plastic. In fact, 99% of plastic is derived from fossil fuels.

And here's the real kicker: as the world (very slowly) transitions to renewable energy and electric cars, the fossil fuel industry is betting on plastic to save them. The International Energy Agency (IEA) projects that by 2050, nearly half of the growth in oil demand will come from petrochemicals, especially plastic.

That's why new plastic plants are still going up. That's why plastic production is expected to triple by 2060. Because when you can't sell oil for gas anymore, you turn it into bags, bottles, cling film, and microbeads. That's the business plan.

And guess what? It's working.

According to the Plastic Waste Makers Index, just 20 companies are responsible for more than half of the world's single-use plastic waste. In 2021, the top three were:

- ExxonMobil

- Dow

- Sinopec (China)

Let that sink in. Three companies, primarily in the business of oil and gas, are at the top of the world's plastic problem. And behind them, a web of banks and governments quietly finances the chaos.

So while you're cutting up six-pack rings and rinsing out peanut butter jars like a good citizen, major institutions are throwing billions at the system to make sure the plastic never stops flowing.

But surely, you think, corporations are feeling the pressure? The public outcry? The turtle with the straw up its nose?

Yes... and no.

They respond with distraction — the great corporate sleight of hand. Coca-Cola announces a new bottle made of "100% recycled plastic" in one city, while quietly pumping out 120 billion plastic bottles a year globally. Nestlé co-founds clean ocean initiatives while fighting for the right to keep bottling spring water in drought-stricken regions. Unilever supports bans on plastic sachets — while continuing to sell billions of them in Southeast Asia because, as one executive put it, "We have to make money."

This isn't hypocrisy. It's strategy.

Companies embrace consumer recycling and cleanups because they know these are solutions that don't threaten their business model. They want you sorting your plastics and feeling hopeful — because the moment you stop believing the myth, the questions get louder:

Why does my shampoo come in three layers of plastic?

Why can't I refill containers?

Why do you produce it, profit from it, and then make me feel guilty for it?

The truth is, plastic is cheap, durable, and disgustingly profitable. It extends shelf life, reduces transport costs, and guarantees repeat purchases. That's why even the "eco" brands still wrap everything like it's being shipped to Mars. The economics are too good to ignore.

But the costs? Oh, they're very real.

They're just not on the balance sheet.

They show up as marine life choked to death in ghost nets. As microplastics lodged in placentas. As mountains of trash poisoning water tables in countries that never asked for our waste in the first place. As cities spending billions to sort trash that shouldn't exist to begin with.

And you, dear citizen, are left trying to patch a hemorrhage with a Band-Aid while the factory keeps churning at full steam.

This isn't just about environmental failure. It's structural betrayal.

The machine is working exactly as intended. Which means if we want to stop drowning in plastic, we need to stop playing the role of unpaid janitor for an industry that won't clean up after itself.

So what now?

Time to talk about alternatives. Real ones.

Not just paper straws and bamboo forks, but rethinking the entire system.

The False Solutions We're Sold

Every great con needs a diversion — something shiny

to keep your eyes off the truth. In the case of plastic pollution, it's not one trick, but a whole circus: biodegradable forks, compostable bags, reusable cups sold in plastic wrap. You've seen them. You've probably bought them. We all have.

Welcome to the theatre of progress.

Let's start with recycling — the original placebo. It's the bedrock of our environmental self-esteem, the ritual we perform to feel better about the avalanche of garbage in which we're complicit. But as we've seen, it doesn't work. Not really.

Most plastic isn't designed to be recycled. It's designed to look recyclable.

Take black plastic, for example. Common in takeout containers and grocery trays — and completely invisible to most optical sorting machines. So it gets trashed. Then there's multi-layered packaging — those chip bags and juice boxes with metal linings sandwiched between plastic and cardboard. They can't be recycled either, but they're still slapped with the comforting triangle of arrows.

Even the plastics that *can* be recycled — PET (#1), HDPE (#2) — lose quality each time they're processed. This is called "downcycling," not recycling. Your bottle doesn't become another bottle. It becomes a

carpet... and then, eventually, garbage. Again.

Then came biodegradable plastics — the next magic trick.

Sounds good, right? Who wouldn't want plastic that just... disappears?

Except it doesn't. Most biodegradable plastics require specific industrial composting conditions: high heat, specific microbes, and tightly controlled environments. Toss them in your backyard compost, or even in many city green bins, and they'll stick around like any other plastic. Some just break into microplastics faster, spreading invisible pollution instead of visible trash.

Same pollution, less guilt. Neat trick.

Reusable shopping bags? On paper, great. But a single cotton tote needs to be used *131 times* to have a lower environmental impact than a plastic one. That's assuming you didn't impulse-buy a dozen "eco-friendly" totes with slogans like *Save the Planet* on them, which then sit in your trunk collecting dust like the graveyard of good intentions they are.

And let's not forget the corporate "solutions." The voluntary sustainability reports. The glossy infographics. The beach cleanups for the cameras. The "recyclable where facilities exist" disclaimers in six-point font. It's all theatre — a stage set to make us feel like the problem is being handled, when in fact, it's only being rebranded.

These aren't solutions. They're symptoms of a deeper dysfunction.

Because here's the ugly truth: we are trying to fix an overproduction problem with end-of-life interventions. That's like trying to end a flood by handing out more buckets.

If your bathtub is overflowing, do you reach for more towels? Or do you turn off the tap?

Yet almost every initiative focuses on cleanup and consumer responsibility, and not on stopping the deluge at its source.

This misdirection isn't accidental. It's orchestrated.

In fact, the entire "Keep America Beautiful" campaign — the birthplace of modern litter-blaming — was funded by companies like Coca-Cola and Dixie Cup. Their goal? To make you think pollution is your fault. Not theirs. It worked brilliantly.

And so we keep buying reusable straws and sorting our plastics and feeling like heroes while global plastic production continues to rise, nearly doubling every 20 years.

The truth is, we cannot consume our way out of this. We cannot shop greener, sort better, or ban straws into salvation. We need a system that produces less waste to begin with.

That begins in the next chapter.

Plastic pollution isn't a glitch in the system — it *is* the system. Despite decades of feel-good recycling campaigns and eco-branding, only a tiny fraction of plastic ever gets truly recycled. The blue bin comforts us, but most plastic ends up in landfills, incinerators, or is dumped overseas. It's a sleight of hand that shifts guilt from the corporations flooding the world with single-use packaging to the consumers desperately trying to "do their part."

Behind the curtain, a small group of petrochemical giants — ExxonMobil, Dow, and others — continue to churn out plastic at record levels. As fossil fuel profits from transportation decline, these companies are doubling down on plastics as their financial future. Banks and governments quietly support this pivot, financing infrastructure that guarantees plastic production will triple by 2060.

Meanwhile, we're sold distractions. Recycling that doesn't really recycle. "Biodegradable" plastics that don't degrade. Eco-products that require more resources to produce than what they replace. It's a circus of false solutions designed to make us feel empowered, while ensuring the Machine keeps running — profitable, polluting, and protected.

A System Built to Fail

You wouldn't need to invent anything new. Just study Canada's system — and replicate it. It's a masterclass in how to build the appearance of environmental responsibility without any of the inconvenient accountability.

On paper, Canada looks like a recycling success story. Blue bins line the curbs of suburban streets. City websites publish colour-coded charts with rules and reminders. School children are taught to sort and rinse, to peel off labels and flatten boxes. We've built an entire civic identity around the idea that we are responsible stewards of our waste.

But scratch the surface and the façade crumbles. The numbers don't add up. The plastics don't get recycled. And the promises made by both industry and government are rarely fulfilled. The truth, hidden behind layers of jargon and PR-friendly statistics, is that the system is broken — and not by accident.

It was designed this way.

What's presented to the public as a sophisticated, coordinated environmental program is, in reality, a Rube Goldberg machine held together with wishful thinking and duct tape. It's a patchwork quilt of fragmented policies, competing jurisdictions, vague standards, and industry-funded optics. Everyone has a role to play — municipalities, provinces, corporations, consumers — but no one actually has control. It's the bureaucratic version of passing the buck in a circle until it disappears.

The result is a system that feels vaguely progressive, even as it fails to deliver on its most basic promises. It's comforting, performative, and deeply misleading.

Think of it like an IKEA cabinet. In the catalogue, it's gorgeous — all clean lines and Nordic charm. But when you open the box, you find 14 missing screws, 3 mismatched panels, and a manual written in abstract symbols. Halfway through, you realize you're missing a hinge and that the wood has already splintered. Eventually, you lean it against a wall, hope no one notices, and call it "done."

That's Canada's recycling system in a nutshell. Shiny on the outside. Unstable underneath.

And the instability is no accident. It's the product of decades of conscious political choices: to underfund the infrastructure, to offload responsibility to municipalities, to let industry set the terms, and to use public goodwill as a substitute for actual results.

What we're dealing with isn't a glitch.

It's a performance.

One that is designed to pacify the public, shift responsibility onto households, and delay meaningful reforms. As long as people believe they're helping — that rinsing a yogurt container and putting it in the right bin is "doing their part" — the deeper structural failures remain invisible. Corporations continue to produce waste with impunity. Governments avoid hard conversations about regulation. And the public keeps playing their role in a game they've been told they can win, even though the rules were rigged from the start.

This isn't just a failed recycling system.

It's a carefully choreographed illusion of one.

The Great Decentralization Scam

If a problem is big, complex, and politically inconvenient, the easiest way to make sure nothing ever gets done about it is to divide it into as many pieces as possible and give each one to someone else. That's not just a tactic — it's Canadian recycling policy.

In theory, environmental protection should be a national priority. But in practice, Canada's recycling system is a fractured mess of overlapping jurisdictions, each doing things their own way, often poorly, and rarely in coordination with one another. The federal government issues polite goals, provinces pass vague legislation, and municipalities are left to actually implement programs — usually with insufficient resources, outdated equipment, and a prayer.

Imagine a national orchestra where each section is told to play whatever piece they want, at whatever tempo they feel like. The result wouldn't be music. It would be noise. That's Canadian recycling — a discordant mix of black bins, blue boxes, green bags, brown composts, bottle deposits, and mysterious "Do Not Recycle" labels that show up with no explanation.

Let's take a simple example. In one city, black plastic isn't recyclable. In another, it sometimes is, depending on the product. In a different one, you're asked to separate certain materials. In other cities, the rules change based on which company won the waste management contract that year. None of this is intuitive, and none of it is made easier by the fact that packaging is designed for marketing appeal, not end-of-life management.

This chaos isn't just frustrating for residents — it's

deliberate.

Because when responsibility is this diluted, accountability becomes impossible. Each level of government can point to another. Each contractor can blame the last one. Each stakeholder — from packaging manufacturers to waste processors — can shrug and say, "Not our fault." And in the end, it's the resident who gets the finger wagged in their face when a greasy pizza box gums up a multi-million-dollar sorting machine.

Worse still, this fragmentation creates a convenient narrative: that the real problem is public ignorance. That if only people sorted better, rinsed more thoroughly, and memorized the local recycling scripture, things would work. But the truth is, no amount of consumer vigilance can fix a system that was never unified in the first place.

A 2020 audit in Ontario found that contamination rates in blue boxes were climbing steadily, but also noted that residents were increasingly confused about the rules. Why wouldn't they be? The rules change from neighbourhood to neighbourhood — and sometimes, from year to year. Residents aren't failing the system. The system is gaslighting the residents.

And this chaos has real consequences.

It means cities spend more on sorting and collection. It means good materials get rejected. It means processing facilities are overburdened and inefficient. And most of all, it means less plastic gets recycled, which, depending on who you ask, might be the point.

The plastic industry has long known that standardizing recycling rules would help boost recovery rates. But they've resisted every meaningful push toward that end. Why? Because better recycling means more scrutiny of packaging, more pressure to design for sustainability, and more talk about banning certain materials altogether.

Fragmentation keeps that conversation from happening. And it allows corporations to keep saying, "We put a recyclable label on it. If it didn't get recycled, that's on you."

So, no — the Great Canadian Recycling Failure isn't just about inefficiency. It's about engineering confusion so thoroughly that it becomes a protective shield for those profiting from the problem.

That's not dysfunction. That's policy by design.

The Economics of Futility

Now, let's talk about the part that moves the system:

money. Or, more accurately, the stubborn, excruciating absence of it — unless you're in the business of making plastic, not cleaning it up.

Municipal recycling budgets are chronically starved. Most recycling programs run on fiscal fumes — balancing spreadsheets that barely cover basics like fleet maintenance and labour, let alone upgrades to aging infrastructure. Trucks are patched together with duct tape and prayer. Optical sorters — the machines that differentiate a milk jug from a salad container — are outdated or broken. And good luck finding consistent funding from the federal level. This isn't a national emergency; it's just garbage, after all.

But that's the rub: this system runs like it's an essential public service, but it behaves like a casino. Recycling is a commodity market. And like any commodity market, it's dictated by global prices, trade disputes, and whatever mood swings the oil industry happens to be having that week.

When oil prices are low, it becomes dirt cheap to produce new, virgin plastic — clean, uniform, and chemically reliable. The recycled stuff? It's suddenly an overpriced substitute. It takes labour to collect, fuel to transport, water and energy to wash, and machines to process — all for a finished product that's less consistent and more expensive than simply starting from scratch. So, guess what happens to your painstakingly rinsed peanut butter jar when oil is cheap?

It dies in a landfill. Quietly. Unceremoniously. Like it never even existed.

Now add market shocks into the equation.

In 2018, China, for years the final destination for Canada's soiled blue bin dreams, shut its doors under the "National Sword" policy. It banned the import of low-grade foreign recyclables, citing contamination and environmental concerns. Translation: your empty ketchup bottle and crumpled clamshell packaging weren't recyclable. They were just well-travelled trash.

The consequences were immediate and severe. Canada's exports of plastic waste dropped by over 90% in one year. Suddenly, all the garbage we thought had magically disappeared across the Pacific started to pile up in our backyards — in warehouses, sorting facilities, and eventually, back in landfills.

In Edmonton, between 2019 and 2020, more than 6,300 tonnes of blue bin materials were quietly trucked to the dump. The city said the material was "not recyclable at the time." Translation: No one wanted to buy it.

In Calgary, plastic film — the stuff your bread and

produce come wrapped in — was sent straight to landfill because processing it wasn't cost-effective.

In Quebec, entire municipalities scrambled to renegotiate or cancel contracts with processors who no longer saw a point in handling low-value plastics.

And then there's Toronto. Canada's largest city, with one of the most robust waste diversion programs in the country, still sees a massive percentage of its plastics end up unrecycled, due not to laziness, but economics. The cost of sorting and processing often exceeds the value of what gets recovered. So the material is triaged. High-value items like clear PET bottles get a second chance. The rest is a financial liability — and it dies in the dark.

This isn't a flaw in the system. This is the system.

It's a shell game, one where municipalities and recycling companies juggle costs and optics while pretending the house isn't on fire. And all of it — the trucks, the bins, the slogans, the Earth Day campaigns — is built on a fragile assumption: that someone, somewhere, wants to buy what we're throwing away.

But plastic waste isn't a product. It's a problem. And problems don't sell well on open markets.

This is why, in moments of honesty, city officials and

recycling coordinators quietly admit that the blue bin is largely symbolic. It's the municipal equivalent of a participation ribbon. We're keeping up appearances, not making a dent.

And corporations? They're only too happy to let it continue. Every time a city tries to regulate or restrict certain types of packaging, the industry shows up with lobbyists and legal threats. Because as long as we keep pretending recycling works, no one has to stop producing garbage.

Even attempts to fix things, like Extended Producer Responsibility (EPR) programs, have been watered down to near uselessness. Loopholes abound. Enforcement is lax. And timelines stretch into the horizon. We're told things will improve in 2026, or 2030, or whenever the next regulation kicks in — assuming it isn't delayed, litigated, or quietly forgotten.

The economics of futility aren't accidental. They are structural, systemic, and staggeringly efficient at doing one thing: keeping the wheels turning while nothing changes.

Until the financial equation changes — until it becomes cheaper to reuse than replace, more profitable to recover than discard — recycling will remain a mirage. A moral placebo. A ritual we perform to distract ourselves from the far more uncomfortable truth:

You can't solve a profit-driven problem with wishful thinking.

A Quietly Engineered Failure

So what's the endgame here? Why build a system so elaborate, so dysfunctional, so hollow?

Because it works. Not at recycling plastic, but at recycling responsibility.

It's a masterclass in misdirection. A system designed less to deal with plastic than to manage public perception of it. It's not broken. It's doing exactly what it was designed to do: delay accountability, shift blame, and kick the can (or bottle, or Styrofoam clamshell) down the road just far enough that no one in power has to feel too bad — or act too soon.

This isn't just about inefficiency or bureaucracy. It's a political product — a tool crafted over decades by lobbyists, consultants, and PR teams to ensure that plastic production can continue without triggering a full-blown public revolt. And it's brilliant, really. Diabolical, but brilliant.

Let's break it down.

Politicians get to wave around high-visibility programs like the Blue Box and declare war on single-use plastics every few years. They pose for photo ops next to piles of recyclables and announce pilot programs with vague promises like "diversion targets" or "zero waste by 2050." By the time anyone notices those targets were missed — or quietly abandoned — the news cycle has moved on.

Corporations, especially the ones that produce the most plastic, get to hide behind a paper-thin curtain of greenwashing. They slap a Möbius triangle on their products, launch sustainability campaigns with soothing music and leafy fonts, and point to municipal recycling systems as proof that their packaging is "responsibly managed." The fine print? Irrelevant. The optics? Immaculate.

Consumers — that's us — get a ritual. A tiny, daily performance of virtue. Rinse the yogurt cup. Sort the bins. Drag them to the curb like a civic offering. And feel good. Feel righteous. You're helping. You're one of the good ones.

And all the while, the machinery behind the curtain quietly collapses under the weight of its own contradiction.

This is environmental theatre at its finest. We're not just the audience. We're the set designers, the performers, and the willing dupes. We buy the tickets, play our part, and applaud on cue. Meanwhile, the real plot — the one where plastic use doubles, triples, then quadruples — plays out offstage, uninterrupted.

The brilliance of this setup is how thoroughly it divides and diffuses responsibility. Every actor in the drama has just enough plausible deniability to avoid blame. Politicians say they've launched initiatives. Corporations say they support recycling. Municipalities say they're doing their best with limited funds. And we, the public, say we've done what we were told.

Nobody's lying outright. Everyone's just selectively honest enough to keep the illusion intact.

And the consequences? They're out of sight. Quite literally. Buried in landfills. Burned in incinerators. Shipped off to developing nations, where children pick through our waste barefoot in open-air dumps. Occasionally, some of it floats back to us — tangled in a turtle's shell, strangling a seabird, or washing up on a beach we thought was pristine.

But by then, it's not *our* fault. It's someone else's. A government failure. A consumer error. A "lack of public education." Never the system. Never the design.

Because if we admitted the system itself is a fraud,

that would mean facing a much darker reality: that real solutions aren't just inconvenient. They're disruptive. They require redesigning of packaging. Restricting certain products. Rethinking the very concept of disposability. And worst of all: they'd cost money — real money, which means someone's profit margin would have to shrink.

And nobody in this theatre wants to be the one who breaks character and says that out loud.

So the performance continues.

We pretend recycling is a solution. Corporations pretend they're sustainable. Governments pretend they're regulating. And once every fortnight, millions of Canadians roll their blue bins to the curb with the faithful resignation of someone offering a sacrifice to a god that never answers.

Because deep down, we know. The ritual doesn't work.

But breaking it? That would mean confronting the truth. And there's nothing less marketable or more necessary than that.

When Solutions Become Threats

The Inconvenient Answer

We are constantly told that plastic pollution is a "complex problem." That it spans supply chains, jurisdictions, and international borders. That it touches everything from oil refining to consumer behaviour to trade agreements. It's always too big. Too expensive. Too messy. Too... convenient to not fix.

But occasionally, someone comes along with a solution that is *not* expensive, *not* complicated, and works. And what happens then?

It gets ignored. Or worse — quietly smothered.

That's the paradox at the heart of environmental policy: the more effective and accessible a solution is, the less welcome it becomes. Not because it's unhelpful, but because it threatens to expose the theatre of inaction that has been so carefully staged. A cheap, fast, replicable idea doesn't just solve a problem — it embarrasses the systems built around pretending to try.

Because if one determined individual or small team can fix what billions in public funds haven't, then what have all those billions bought us? Advisory panels? Awareness campaigns? Plastic education week?

Imagine, for instance, a community project that installs inexpensive plastic catchment systems along stormwater drains. It stops microplastics from washing into rivers and costs under $5,000 per unit. Suddenly, municipalities spending tens of millions on pilot programs and five-year feasibility studies start looking like they're burning money. The community team becomes a nuisance. They're too effective. They highlight inefficiency.

A real solution — one that circumvents bureaucracy and delivers impact — doesn't look like progress. It looks like mutiny.

And that's what makes it dangerous.

Because entrenched systems aren't designed to *solve* problems — they're designed to *manage* them, slowly, with great ceremony, and always just enough to justify another round of funding. The whole ecosystem — bureaucrats, consultants, NGOs, private contractors — survives on the continued existence of the problem. Solutions that truly work threaten everyone's job security.

That's why new ideas often aren't judged on their merit. They're judged on their disruptiveness. The more they stand to shift the balance of power, the more likely they are to be buried under words like "premature," "unsanctioned," or "not evidence-based" — bureaucratic speak for *go away*.

This is the uncomfortable truth: if your solution doesn't fit neatly into a 200-page action plan with a government logo on the cover, it doesn't matter how effective it is. The system won't see it as help. It will see it as competition.

Because no one wants to be made obsolete — especially not by someone without a title, a committee, or a million-dollar grant. Especially not by someone who just went out and *did the thing*.

So the myth continues: that we need more time, more data, more alignment, more oversight. That the problem is just too complicated to fix quickly.

But often, the real obstacle isn't the problem. It's the people who benefit from pretending to solve it.

The Cost of Letting Bureaucracies "Lead" Innovation

We've all seen what happens when bureaucracies are put in charge of innovation: they hold a press conference, form a task force, and then go into a two-year period of introspection. Nothing happens — but it happens in triplicate.

Governments are not designed to innovate. They are designed to manage risk, mitigate liability, and avoid blame. This makes them excellent at producing memos, mediocre at implementing change, and downright allergic to anything resembling agility.

Innovation, on the other hand, thrives on uncertainty. It requires speed, risk, failure, and iteration — four things government systems find morally offensive. In bureaucratic culture, failure is something to be avoided at all costs. But in real innovation, failure is fuel. You learn, adjust, and improve. Bureaucracy doesn't fail fast. It fails quietly, then gets a budget increase.

Let's say you pitch a novel idea to a government ministry — something bold, practical, and disruptive. What happens? It gets reviewed by a committee. Then passed to another committee. Then redirected to a "cross-ministerial working group." By the time it's presented to a deputy minister, the idea has been sanded down, stripped of urgency, and wrapped in enough jargon to make sure nobody understands it.

And if it somehow *does* get approved? Get ready for procurement hell. You'll spend eighteen months filling out forms to prove you're not a Russian bot before you can order a screwdriver. The system does not move fast. It moves officially.

There's a reason most truly impactful innovations in the environmental space — from community composting networks to plastic interception technology — start outside of government. Bureaucracies only adopt ideas once they're proven successful *somewhere else*, by someone else, using someone else's money.

Why? Because risk is political poison. A government trying something new that doesn't work? That's a headline. A government not trying at all? That's Tuesday.

In many cases, governments *wait* for grassroots groups, researchers, or startups to do the hard part: to test, refine, and prove the model. Then, if it looks safe enough, and if the media heat gets a little too high, they swoop in, stamp their logo on it, and announce a pilot project for a smaller version of the thing that already works.

It's not entirely malicious. It's just the nature of institutions. They weren't built to sprint. They were built to survive. And in that sense, they're doing exactly what they were designed to do: protect themselves from disruption, even when that disruption is desperately needed.

This is the cost of letting bureaucracy lead innovation: we move slowly, we move cautiously, and sometimes, we don't move at all. The plastic piles up. The emissions rise. The oceans choke. But the paperwork? Impeccable.

The Ocean Cleanup Analogy: Innovation vs. Institutions

In 2013, a teenage Dutch inventor named Boyan Slat stood on a TEDx stage with a question that seemed too obvious to ask: "Why don't we just clean up the ocean?" It was the kind of idea experts had long dismissed as naive, too difficult, or economically unfeasible. But instead of being paralyzed by institutional inertia, Slat went to work.

He dropped out of university, built a team, and crowdfunded millions. Within a few years, he had deployed the first large-scale passive plastic collection system in the Great Pacific Garbage Patch — the first of its kind. It didn't require international treaties. It didn't require government departments. It didn't need years of roundtable diplomacy. It just needed someone to say: "Let's build the damn thing."

Compare that to how governments have dealt with ocean plastic over the same period: workshops, white papers, awareness campaigns, and a lot of very serious-looking people sitting in very expensive rooms talking about what should *eventually* be done. Meanwhile, a 16-year-old beat them to it.

And let's be clear: the Ocean Cleanup project isn't perfect. The first few deployments failed. The technology is still evolving. But the point isn't that they got it exactly right — it's that they did it at all. They tried. They learned. They improved. They acted.

This is the schism at the heart of environmental action: individuals innovate; institutions hesitate.

When a citizen launches a radical idea, they're often treated as a fringe idealist. When an institution fails to act, it's chalked up to "complexity." The same governments that applaud climate marches and publish glossy "green" plans will often ignore — or worse, undermine — grassroots solutions that don't fit their frameworks or funding models.

Why? Because success outside the system exposes the system. If a kid from the Netherlands can do in five years what the UN hasn't done in fifty, then what does that say about all the committees, budgets, and grandstanding?

The Ocean Cleanup isn't just a technological achievement. It's a mirror held up to the world's most powerful institutions, asking: "What's your excuse?"

And that's why real innovation often happens on the margins — not in ministries or boardrooms, but in basements, garages, and co-working spaces. It's where problems get solved because someone cares more about the outcome than the optics.

The message is simple and threatening: If you won't fix it, we will.

Innovation Is Welcome — Until It Works

Governments love innovation, as long as it doesn't work.

That may sound cynical, but it's backed up by pattern after pattern of real-world failure, not of technology, but of adoption. Politicians, department heads, and agency spokespeople all have the same playbook: champion innovation, fund studies, host conferences, and hire consultants. But when something disruptive *delivers* — when it threatens to outperform the complex, bloated, grant-dependent machine, the system clutches its pearls.

Why? Because functioning outside the system is the gravest sin in a system built to perpetuate itself. A small, efficient, fast-moving solution is not seen as an opportunity. It's seen as an existential threat.

Innovation That Works Is Politically Inconvenient

When a tiny team solves a giant problem, it shows up everyone with more power, money, and resources. It calls into question the necessity of expensive infrastructure, bureaucratic oversight, and multi-year pilot projects. If someone with a $10,000 idea can do what your $6 billion task force hasn't, what exactly have you been doing all this time?

This is why many of the most transformative environmental innovations had to succeed outside of government before anyone inside it took them seriously. Let's look at some of the clearest case studies.

Case Study 1: The Ocean Cleanup (Boyan Slat, Netherlands)

In 2013, 16-year-old Boyan Slat proposed a bold, almost childishly simple idea: Why not use ocean currents themselves to passively gather the plastic that's already floating in the Pacific?

At first, he was ignored. Then he was laughed at. Marine scientists told him it couldn't work. NGOs accused him of distracting from source reduction. Governments declined to help. After all, who was this teenager without a PhD, a ministerial title, or a UN grant?

So Slat crowdfunded millions online. He built prototypes. He tested in the North Sea and eventually deployed a full-scale interceptor in the Great Pacific Garbage Patch. By 2021, his system had successfully removed tens of thousands of kilograms of ocean plastic. He followed that with a river-interception system targeting the top plastic-polluting waterways, where 80% of ocean plastic originates.

And now? Countries and corporations are taking notice. But only after years of ridicule and inaction.

Lesson: The system only wants your idea *after* it's bulletproof. Until then, it will undermine, ignore, or sideline you — often to protect its own image.

Case Study 2: Terracycle (Tom Szaky, USA/Canada)

Tom Szaky's startup began with the idea of packaging fertilizer in used soda bottles. It evolved into Terracycle, a global enterprise that handles waste streams too "difficult" for traditional recyclers: cigarette butts, chip bags, cosmetic tubes, toothbrushes.

Terracycle doesn't wait for municipalities. It builds direct partnerships with brands like Colgate, L'Oréal, and Nestlé, creating prepaid programs where consumers can mail in their "unrecyclables." It also created the Loop initiative — a zero-waste delivery system using refillable packaging.

Despite proven success, many cities refuse to adapt or integrate Terracycle into their official waste systems. The reason? Terracycle works outside the municipal contract model. It doesn't rely on taxpayers. It doesn't fit neatly into a city's procurement policy.

Lesson: Success, when achieved through private agility, is treated not as inspiration but as subversion.

Case Study 3: Precious Plastic (Dave Hakkens, Netherlands)

Dutch designer Dave Hakkens developed Precious Plastic, a modular, open-source platform that allows anyone to build small-scale plastic recycling machines with basic tools and scrap metal. His blueprints are available online for free. Thousands of DIY recycling hubs now exist globally, many in underserved communities or regions where industrial recycling is non-existent.

The idea was revolutionary: *empower local people to turn trash into goods — chairs, tiles, phone cases, you name it.*

But Precious Plastic never received widespread institutional support. Governments didn't adopt it. Municipal programs didn't promote it. Why? Because it undermines the scale and exclusivity of government-controlled recycling.

Lesson: Empowerment that bypasses bureaucracy is seen as dangerous, even if it works better.

Case Study 4: Lufa Farms (Montreal, Canada)

Lufa Farms builds commercial rooftop greenhouses on buildings in the city, growing food year-round with hydroponic systems that use 90% less water, no new land, and very few transport miles. They deliver fresh produce to subscribers' doors within hours of harvest, drastically reducing the carbon footprint of industrial agriculture.

It's the kind of green innovation cities claim to love. But Montreal offered no tax break, no regulatory carve-out, and no fast-track zoning process. Lufa had to push through red tape on its own, and still thrives

without the city's help.

Why the cold shoulder? Because it bypasses large-scale infrastructure and centralized food systems, and proves that those systems might not be as necessary as we think.

Lesson: Solutions that decentralize power and reduce dependency are often ignored or actively discouraged.

Why This Pattern Matters

When governments reject good ideas, they don't say, *"This would make us look bad."* They say:

- "It's not scalable."

- "It needs further study."

- "There are safety/regulatory concerns."

- "We're already exploring alternatives."

- "It's outside our jurisdiction."

But behind these platitudes is a quiet truth: a system designed to protect itself will never embrace ideas that threaten its relevance.

And so the same cycle repeats:

- The press celebrates a new grant, not a working prototype.

- Bureaucrats protect budgets, not outcomes.

- Committees discuss problems that scrappy inventors have already solved.

Real innovation — the kind that makes entire departments unnecessary — is welcomed only when it's too big to ignore.

Until then, it's treated like a virus.

The DIY Future

If the system won't save us, we'll save ourselves.

If you want to glimpse the future of environmental solutions, don't look to a summit or ministerial press release. Look for the tinkerers in shipping containers, the teenagers coding in their bedrooms, the farmers hacking old motors, and the communities digging their own trenches when no help comes.

The next wave of climate resilience is being engineered in silence. It's improvised. It's messy. And it works.

The Rise of Guerrilla Sustainability

Faced with institutional indifference, individuals and small groups around the world are stepping into the void. They're not waiting for funding, approval, or applause. They're doing the thing — right now, in spite of the rules.

In Indonesia, local communities along the Citarum River — one of the world's most polluted waterways — began hand-collecting plastic waste and installing homemade filtration barriers from bamboo and mesh long before the government acknowledged the crisis. Their makeshift systems are simple, cheap, and prevent thousands of kilograms of waste from reaching the ocean each year.

In Kenya, teenager Nzambi Matee started her company *Gjenge Makers* after getting frustrated with plastic waste clogging up the streets. With no formal engineering background, she developed a process to turn discarded plastic into durable paving bricks — stronger than concrete and made for less than $10 per square meter. Her small team now produces over 1,000 bricks a day, creating jobs and reducing landfill use without a cent of state investment.

In Beirut, after a garbage crisis left refuse rotting in the streets, local residents formed cooperatives to build small-scale composting and recycling stations in their neighbourhoods. With homemade sorting tables and scavenged containers, they created an informal waste diversion system that outperformed the city's paralyzed infrastructure.

In rural India, women's collectives like *SELCO Foundation* have taken power into their own hands — literally. They build and maintain decentralized solar microgrids in villages that government programs have long ignored. These systems power lights, irrigation pumps, and health clinics — all without waiting for a utility company to show up.

None of these initiatives were part of a national plan. All of them work.

The Power of Open Source

One of the most radical aspects of this movement is its refusal to hoard knowledge.

Projects like Precious Plastic have democratized the ability to recycle by providing free blueprints for DIY machines that shred, melt, and mould plastic into new products. Today, there are over 400 active Precious Plastic workspaces around the world — from Ghana to Ukraine — each adapting the machines to local needs and waste streams.

In Brazil, Favela communities use shared open-source

air quality sensors (developed by grassroots tech group *Open Environmental Data Project*) to monitor pollution levels. These sensors are cheaper and more responsive than the government's, and the data collected has helped challenge official narratives on industrial emissions.

In Palestine, where movement restrictions make it difficult to import goods, local innovators share 3D printer designs for medical equipment and water filtration tools through online repositories. These aren't just hacks — they're lifelines.

This open-source approach accelerates impact. Instead of guarding intellectual property, these projects treat knowledge as a collective inheritance — one that becomes more powerful each time it's copied, modified, and improved.

Why Bureaucracies Hate This

Institutions thrive on control. DIY movements do not.

When a neighbourhood creates its own compost system or water purification device, it circumvents regulation, procurement contracts, and long-standing consulting relationships. These informal systems don't follow protocol. They don't generate the right paperwork. And they don't need permission.

Which is exactly why they're so often shut down.

- In London, guerrilla gardeners planting vegetables on neglected public land were fined for unauthorized land use, even though their work beautified urban spaces and fed local families.

- In Melbourne, an urban fridge project — allowing residents to share surplus food anonymously — was dismantled due to "public safety concerns" despite zero incidents reported.

- In Toronto, a self-built composting system in a low-income neighbourhood was forced to shut down because it didn't comply with waste management by-laws — the same by-laws the city had failed to enforce for corporate polluters.

The real message behind these shutdowns is clear: *It's not a solution unless we control it.*

But that's changing.

The Unruly Future

Across the globe, more people are coming to a shared realization: the cavalry isn't coming. And rather than surrender to despair, they're building their own cavalry out of whatever tools, scraps, and knowledge they can find.

These DIY solutions are messy. They aren't scalable in the traditional sense. But they work, they adapt, and they spread — not because they've been approved, but because they're necessary.

And as climate crises intensify and institutions continue to stall, these bottom-up movements may be our best — and perhaps only — chance at meaningful resilience.

The Real Barriers to Change

It's not the plastic. It's the politics.

When people ask why the world hasn't solved the plastic problem, the answers usually fall into technical categories: lack of infrastructure, insufficient technology, poor consumer behaviour, or economic feasibility. But dig deeper, and the real roadblocks aren't physical. They're human — and often, institutional.

We have the tools. What we lack is permission.

The Power of Inertia

Institutions are designed to preserve themselves.

Change — especially the kind that challenges their relevance — is perceived as a threat, not a goal. This is why bureaucracies tend to absorb reform efforts like a swamp absorbs a rock: they slow it, surround it, and eventually bury it.

When a new idea enters the system, the reflex is often to study it to death. Create a task force. Commission a white paper. Send it through "stakeholder engagement." By the time the idea emerges again — if it does at all — it's been diluted beyond recognition.

Case in point: Canada's 2018 announcement to "ban single-use plastics." It made headlines. It boosted poll numbers. But it was followed by years of consultation, lobbying, and fine print that quietly excluded the most common forms of plastic waste. When the regulations finally came into force, they were so riddled with exceptions and loopholes that little changed. Plastic straws may have disappeared, but plastic wrappers, films, and containers — the bulk of consumer waste — stayed untouched.

This is not failure by accident. It's failure by design.

Lobbyists in the Room

It's no secret that the fossil fuel and plastic industries are deeply embedded in policymaking. In Canada alone, oil and gas lobbyists logged over 1,700 meetings with federal officials in just one year. Many of those meetings were about "plastics management."

These companies don't need to win every argument. They just need to delay action long enough to keep operating at full capacity. Every year of stalled regulation means another year of profit.

A 2021 investigation by *The Guardian* revealed that major plastic producers like Dow Chemical and ExxonMobil were behind public campaigns touting recycling, not because they believed in it, but because it was the best way to fend off regulation. If people think plastics are recyclable, they'll keep buying them. And governments won't ban them.

The result is a masterclass in deflection: shift responsibility from producer to consumer, from design to disposal. You're not polluting because they made garbage. You're polluting because you didn't sort it properly.

The Fear of Simplicity

There's an unspoken assumption in policymaking that complex problems require complex solutions. The idea that something as massive as plastic pollution could be addressed through straightforward, low-tech interventions is almost offensive to the institutional ego.

Why fund a local entrepreneur building biodegradable packaging when you've just announced a multi-billion-dollar innovation hub for "sustainable materials research"? Why support a DIY repair co-op when your city has just signed a ten-year exclusive waste contract with a multinational conglomerate?

Simplicity is threatening because it exposes inefficiency. It strips away the pretense of progress and reveals how bloated and self-serving the existing systems really are.

The Public Performance of Concern

Perhaps the most insidious barrier to change is the illusion that change is already happening.

Every Earth Day press release. Every blue bin on the curb. Every corporate pledge to go "net-zero by 2050." These symbols create the perception of motion. They act as a sedative, convincing people that someone else is handling the problem.

Meanwhile, global plastic production continues to rise. Waste is burned in poor communities. Marine ecosystems collapse. But the optics are good, and in politics, optics often outweigh outcomes.

Governments don't need to fix the problem, they just need to look like they're trying.

The True Cost of Avoidance

What we're really dealing with is a system that fears accountability more than it fears collapse.

It would rather spend billions managing symptoms — landfilling waste, subsidizing oil, cleaning beaches — than confront the root cause: an economic model that treats endless consumption as a virtue and waste as someone else's problem.

Real change would mean confronting powerful industries, disrupting international trade, rewriting procurement rules, and admitting that decades of "recycling" policy were largely performative. That's a lot to ask from institutions that can barely agree on the colour of a reusable bag.

But until we acknowledge these real barriers — and stop pretending the problem is technical — we're doomed to keep chasing our tails in an expensive circle.

The Recycling Myth Machine

How a False Solution Became a Global Belief System

Recycling is the environmental fairy tale we grew up with — the bedtime story that soothes our consumer guilt and lets us sleep at night. It's our moral escape hatch. We're told that as long as we put the "right things" in the "right bin," we are doing our part. The rest — the messy industrial process — will take care of itself. The bottle becomes a park bench, the yogurt cup is reincarnated as a flowerpot, and the planet is spared another wound.

It's a seductive story. And it's a lie.

At its core, the modern recycling narrative was not born from grassroots activism or environmental science — it was a marketing strategy. A coordinated, top-down invention developed and funded by industries whose business models depended on disposability. Plastic producers, beverage giants, packaging corporations, and petrochemical lobbyists needed a way to deflect criticism without changing the fundamentals of their operations. Recycling was their fig leaf — a palatable half-truth that gave consumers comfort, politicians cover, and companies a license to continue profiting from pollution.

What began as a limited municipal experiment quickly grew into a global ideology, embedded in classrooms, governments, and households around the world. Over the past five decades, it has morphed into what can only be described as a secular belief system — complete with rituals (rinsing, sorting, binning), sacred symbols (the chasing arrows), and an unshakable faith in redemption. We don't just do recycling — we believe in it.

This belief, however, is not based on the effectiveness of recycling itself. It's based on a manufactured narrative — a clever distortion of responsibility, engineered to make pollution seem like a behavioural problem rather than a production one. We are told that the issue lies with careless individuals who fail to recycle properly, not with the corporations that churn out billions of non-recyclable products every year.

And it worked.

In North America and Europe, the recycling story became so embedded in public consciousness that questioning it feels like heresy. In classrooms, children are taught to recycle as a civic duty. In public policy, recycling targets are paraded as environmental achievements. In corporate boardrooms, sustainability reports trumpet recycling rates while production of virgin plastic continues to rise year after year.

The result is a global consensus built on magical thinking — that we can consume endlessly, package everything, and still avert ecological disaster as long as we toss things in the right bin.

This isn't just a failure of policy. It's a cultural delusion.

The deeper danger is that this myth actively blocks better solutions. It distracts from upstream fixes like reducing plastic production, regulating packaging, and investing in reuse systems. As long as people believe recycling works, there is no pressure to change the system that keeps producing the waste in the first place.

To dismantle this belief system is not simply about correcting a public misconception — it's about liberating environmental progress from a decades-long trap. It requires confronting the industries that benefit from the illusion, the governments that have leaned on it for political convenience, and the consumers who have come to see it as part of their moral identity.

This chapter unpacks how this false solution became a dominant global narrative — how it was built, who keeps it alive, and why we must confront it head-on if we're serious about solving the environmental crises it was designed to hide.

The Birth of a Narrative

The myth of recycling wasn't born in a lab or a town hall. It was born in a boardroom.

By the 1970s, public consciousness around environmental issues was rising. Rivers were catching fire, smog blanketed major cities, and landfills were starting to overflow. The first Earth Day in 1970 drew 20 million Americans to the streets. The message was clear: pollution wasn't just an eyesore — it was a threat to health, ecosystems, and the moral integrity of modern life.

For the plastics industry, this was an existential threat. The miracle material of the postwar boom — once hailed for its affordability, durability, and convenience — was now becoming a symbol of environmental decay. Photos of plastic bags fluttering in trees, six-pack rings strangling turtles, and disposable packaging choking waterways began to dominate public discourse.

The response from industry was not to change the

product, but to change the narrative.

Instead of accepting restrictions, regulations, or a redesign of their business model, plastics manufacturers embarked on a campaign of strategic misdirection. Their core strategy was disarmingly simple: convince the public that plastic waste isn't a production issue — it's a disposal issue. And even more specifically, that it's your disposal issue.

It was during this time that the "chasing arrows" symbol was introduced, a design lifted from the broader environmental movement and repurposed to serve corporate ends. It first appeared as part of an initiative by the Society of the Plastics Industry (SPI) in 1988, not to signify recyclability, but to code the type of resin used in a plastic product. It was never a recycling guarantee. But the visual trickery — a triangle made of arrows, visually echoing the universal recycling logo — created the desired confusion.

Suddenly, nearly every piece of plastic carried the comforting image of circularity, no matter how obscure or economically unviable it was to actually recycle. Whether it was a yogurt lid made from #5 polypropylene or a black plastic tray coated in food residue, the mere presence of arrows signalled virtue.

In reality, most of these items were not recyclable in any practical sense — either because of contamination, material complexity, or lack of infrastructure. But the illusion worked.

By the early 1990s, the American Plastics Council (funded by industry heavyweights like Dow, Exxon, and DuPont) had launched a multimillion-dollar PR blitz. Television ads, school education kits, magazine spreads — all preaching the gospel of recycling. The messaging was uniform and aggressive: *Plastics are valuable. Plastics are endlessly recyclable. You, the consumer, just need to do your part.*

Behind the scenes, lobbyists fought tooth and nail against legislation that would have forced companies to reduce plastic use, develop alternatives, or implement producer responsibility schemes. In public, they waved the recycling flag.

This sleight of hand worked brilliantly. It reframed the issue entirely. No longer was the plastics industry on trial — now, individual consumers were being judged for not recycling "correctly." Waste became a matter of personal virtue, not systemic design.

The same playbook soon spread globally.

In Canada, industry groups adopted similar messaging in the 1990s and 2000s. The Canadian Plastics Industry Association (CPIA) ran campaigns praising the "lightweight, efficient, recyclable" nature of plastics, while quietly resisting calls for extended producer responsibility (EPR). Municipalities were left to foot the bill for increasingly complex and contaminated waste streams.

And the illusion deepened. Recycling bins multiplied. Municipal programs expanded. Yet recycling rates, especially for plastics, remained anemic. As of 2021, Canada recycled only about 9% of its plastic waste. The rest went to landfills, incinerators, or were shipped abroad — often under the guise of "recyclable exports," a euphemism for waste dumping in poorer countries.

This wasn't an accident. It was a success story for the industry.

By constructing a narrative architecture around recycling — symbols, slogans, school programs, municipal partnerships — the plastics industry delayed regulatory action for decades. It allowed producers to churn out trillions of single-use items while blaming the public for the mess.

And perhaps the most diabolical part? They made us believe we were the heroes of the story.

The Ritualization of Responsibility

Recycling didn't just become a habit — it became a ritual, a kind of environmental sacrament in modern life. Over time, it adopted all the trappings of a belief system: sacred symbols, repeated gestures, a sense of personal redemption, and the comforting illusion of moral participation in a vast, chaotic world.

It starts innocently. You rinse the yogurt cup. Peel off the lid. Pause to squint at the number stamped in the chasing arrows. You debate whether the greasy pizza box counts as paper or trash. You open the blue bin, deposit your offering, and close the lid — lighter, relieved, slightly more virtuous.

This isn't just behaviour. It's ritualized hope.

And like any good ritual, its power lies in repetition, not results.

Most people can't track what happens to their recyclables after they leave the curb, nor are they encouraged to. What matters is the action, not the outcome. The system, however broken, is shielded by a kind of collective faith. We rarely ask tough questions about efficiency, market demand, or material recovery rates. We don't want to know if the black plastic tray is incinerated or if the bag of shredded paper gets sent to the landfill. We just want

to feel like we tried.

This process of ritualization was not accidental — it was carefully nurtured.

The recycling bin became a kind of modern confessional. It turned environmental harm into a solvable moral problem. It offered an answer to the guilt of overconsumption, packaging excess, and fossil-fuel dependency. The equation was simple: keep buying, just throw it in the right bin.

This transformation was supported by advertising, school curricula, government brochures, and even product packaging that weaponized moral language: "100% recyclable," "eco-friendly," "do your part." These aren't technical descriptions — they're invitations to a secular religion of cleanliness and redemption.

And the power of this system is evident in one simple fact:
Even when people know it doesn't work, they keep doing it.

Environmental scholars call this phenomenon "moral licensing" — the idea that performing a good act (like recycling) gives individuals psychological permission to engage in less virtuous behaviour elsewhere (like excessive consumption). The recycling bin becomes a moral offset. It allows people to ignore the bigger problem: why so much waste is being produced in the first place.

A 2019 study from the University of Georgia found that consumers buy more plastic-packaged products when those products are labelled as recyclable, even if recycling rates for those materials are extremely low. The ritual reassures. The facts are inconvenient.

And this isn't just a North American issue.

In Japan, where waste-sorting regulations are among the strictest in the world, residents sometimes sort garbage into more than 40 categories. Compliance is high, but actual recycling rates still depend on international markets, incinerators, and fossil fuels. The system is driven as much by social conformity and ritualized behaviour as by environmental efficacy.

In Germany, often hailed as a recycling champion, citizens proudly sort their waste into multiple colored bins. Yet the country is also one of the largest exporters of plastic waste, a portion of which ends up in Southeast Asian landfills or waterways. The ritual remains intact, even if the system offloads the consequences elsewhere.

What we're left with is a kind of eco-performance: a deeply ingrained script that we follow not because it's effective, but because we've been conditioned to believe that *not* doing it is irresponsible, even shameful.

And that's the mark of a truly successful myth:
Even after the data collapses, the behaviour persists.

The Industry of Distraction

Recycling is not just a misunderstood solution — it has become a full-fledged industry of distraction, one that profits from keeping us focused on the wrong problem.

While we busy ourselves sorting bottle caps and rinsing peanut butter jars, the companies producing the majority of plastic pollution continue to manufacture waste at record levels. This is not a coincidence. It's a design.

Behind the ritual of recycling lies a carefully engineered ecosystem of non-solutions — PR campaigns, third-party certifications, and corporate-sponsored "initiatives" that give the appearance of progress while changing absolutely nothing. These distractions are not side effects of the system. They are the system.

Greenwashing as Strategy

The term *greenwashing* was coined in the 1980s, but

it's become a dominant tactic in the decades since. Corporations invest millions into marketing that paints them as part of the solution, even as their core business model relies on exponential plastic production.

Take Coca-Cola, which has been named the world's worst plastic polluter five years in a row by Break Free From Plastic audits. Despite this, the company touts its commitment to a "World Without Waste," complete with recyclable bottles and plastic offset programs. Meanwhile, it produces over 100 billion plastic bottles annually — none of which are truly circular, and many of which end up in the environment.

Or consider Nestlé, which launched an "eco-friendly" water brand called *Pure Life* that came in recyclable plastic bottles — even though its overall environmental footprint, from bottle manufacturing to shipping and extraction, remained damaging. Nestlé publicly supports recycling infrastructure while lobbying against stronger packaging regulations across Europe and North America.

The same applies to oil and petrochemical giants. ExxonMobil, Chevron, and Shell have heavily promoted plastic recycling since the 1980s, all while continuing to expand their plastic production capacity. Why? Because plastic, made from petroleum byproducts, is their growth strategy in a decarbonizing world. If the public believed plastic could be infinitely recycled, there would be less pressure to ban, tax, or reduce it.

The Role of Industry-Funded NGOs

To shield themselves further, many corporations create or fund front groups and non-profits that appear neutral, scientific, or public-interest driven. These include organizations like:

- The Alliance to End Plastic Waste — a coalition of petrochemical companies promoting technological fixes like "chemical recycling" while resisting regulatory bans.

- Keep America Beautiful — originally launched by packaging and beverage companies to shift the focus of waste from producers to "litterbugs" (i.e., individuals).

- How2Recycle — a labelling initiative that uses standardized recycling symbols, even when many labelled products are not recyclable in most facilities.

These groups do not challenge the production of waste. Instead, they focus on *managing* it — rebranding trash, reframing consumer habits, and rechanneling public outrage into manageable gestures.

Science at Arm's Length

Corporate influence doesn't stop at messaging. It extends to academic research, where studies are funded to highlight new "innovations" in recycling, from biodegradable plastics that rarely degrade to high-tech sorting systems that are too expensive to scale.

This creates the illusion of progress. We are told that the problem is being handled. That solutions are "on the horizon." That we just need a little more funding, a little more innovation, a little more time.

But these promises rarely materialize into action. The real goal isn't to solve plastic pollution — it's to delay meaningful regulation by keeping hope alive.

The Price of Distraction

The industry of distraction isn't harmless. Every dollar spent on hollow campaigns and PR-driven "solutions" is a dollar not spent on prevention, reuse systems, or plastic alternatives. Every year we waste on myth maintenance is a year of increased pollution and community harm.

And most dangerously, this system conditions us to believe that the responsibility lies with *us*, not with the corporations flooding the planet with single-use waste.

The more we buy into the illusion, the less likely we are to demand real change.

Media, Messaging, and Manufactured Consent

The story of recycling didn't spread by accident. It was strategically seeded and relentlessly repeated. Over decades, media outlets, government agencies, and even schools participated in creating a kind of civic religion — one in which recycling wasn't just encouraged but morally imperative.

The Power of Repetition

In television ads, billboards, cereal box cartoons, and government pamphlets, the message was simple and uniform: *"Reduce, reuse, recycle."* But over time, that message narrowed into just one word: recycle. Reducing and reusing were too disruptive to business. Recycling, on the other hand, was compatible with consumption — it let people keep buying while feeling responsible.

Children's programming like *Captain Planet*, *Sesame Street*, and *Schoolhouse Rock* incorporated recycling into their storylines. Public service announcements, often sponsored by industry groups, flooded airwaves with images of happy families sorting their waste while cheerful music played in the background.

Recycling became not just a habit, but a cultural ritual, embedded in early education and reinforced throughout adulthood.

Meanwhile, media coverage largely avoided the cracks in the system. Articles about the success of new recycling programs, upgrades to sorting facilities, or citizen "green heroes" were far more common than deep dives into what actually happened to the material once collected. The coverage was overwhelmingly positive, and often based on press releases from municipal governments or industry groups.

This was not an oversight. It was a form of manufactured consent, where media, knowingly or not, legitimized a system designed to deflect scrutiny and avoid systemic reform.

Industry's Invisible Hand

At the centre of this narrative management was the plastics and oil industry. As early as the 1970s, industry groups began to fund studies, lobby governments, and work with PR firms to craft a message that emphasized consumer responsibility. Their goal: protect profits by distracting from production.

This campaign peaked in the 1990s, when organizations like the American Plastics Council and Keep America Beautiful poured millions into advertising campaigns. These efforts helped place the now-ubiquitous "chasing arrows" symbol on plastic products, even though most of them were not recyclable in any practical sense. The symbol wasn't regulated. It was marketing dressed up as environmentalism.

Keep America Beautiful, one of the most influential groups in this space, presents itself as a nonprofit civic group. In reality, it was co-founded by Coca-Cola and other beverage companies to shift public focus from the waste their products created to the supposed irresponsibility of consumers. Their iconic 1971 "Crying Indian" commercial — still one of the most recognized environmental ads in history — perfectly captured this deflection. The message wasn't "companies must stop flooding the market with waste." It was "you, the litterbug, are the problem."

The Exposés That Shook the Myth

When journalists have attempted to pierce this manufactured reality, the results have been jarring. A 2020 investigation by NPR and PBS Frontline revealed internal documents showing that industry leaders knew as early as the 1970s that plastic recycling would never work at scale — that it was too expensive, too complicated, and too limited in scope. But instead of changing course, they doubled down on recycling as a public-facing solution.

The public reaction to this report was mixed. Some were outraged. Others were simply numb. The idea that recycling — an act synonymous with environmental responsibility — was a knowingly false promise was too much to absorb.

This is the power of myth. Even when the facts are exposed, the belief lingers. People would rather continue the comforting ritual than confront the scale of deception. This cognitive dissonance is precisely what the original campaign intended to exploit. If recycling is exposed as a sham, then we are forced to reckon not just with our own habits, but also with decades of misplaced trust in corporations, governments, and institutions.

Silence Is Strategic

Today, even as more evidence emerges of the limits and failures of recycling, mainstream coverage remains cautious. Articles often mention "challenges" or "barriers" but rarely call out the foundational lie: that recycling was never meant to solve plastic pollution, only to make it look like someone else's problem.

This silence is not accidental. Challenging the recycling myth means challenging an entire economic model — one built on disposability, convenience, and externalized costs. It means asking uncomfortable questions about power, profit, and complicity. And that's a story the media, too often reliant on advertising revenue from the very companies responsible, has been slow to tell.

The Corporate Shield

Recycling has become the perfect alibi for corporate pollution. It allows companies to continue flooding the world with single-use plastics while appearing environmentally responsible. This isn't accidental — it's strategic.

For multinational giants like Coca-Cola, Nestlé, PepsiCo, Unilever, and others, the narrative of recycling serves one primary function: deflection. By focusing public attention on waste management and consumer habits, these companies shift the spotlight away from the sheer volume of plastic they produce. They champion recycling not because it works, but because it works for them, as public relations, not environmental protection.

Recyclable ≠ Recycled

One of the most misleading tactics is the corporate obsession with "recyclable" packaging. Many companies boast that their bottles, wrappers, or containers are now "100% recyclable." But that label often means little in practice.

Take multilayer sachets, widely used across India and Southeast Asia to package everything from shampoo to snacks. These packets are technically "recyclable" — in theory. But in practice, their complex layering of plastic, foil, and adhesives makes them nearly impossible to recycle with conventional equipment. India generates over 20,000 tonnes of plastic waste daily, much of it from single-use packaging that can't be recycled economically, yet bears the recycling symbol anyway.

In the U.S., municipal recycling systems routinely reject items marked as recyclable by brands. For example, plastic clamshell containers (like those used for berries) are accepted in less than 30% of curbside recycling programs, despite being labelled recyclable.

This disconnect isn't a bug — it's a feature. The "chasing arrows" symbol, which most consumers interpret as a certification of recyclability, was never meant to guarantee recycling. It was introduced in the 1980s as a marketing tool, not a recycling standard.

The result? Consumers feel good about their purchases, while companies avoid accountability.

Token Programs and Green Partnerships

To keep public pressure at bay, many corporations launch high-profile but low-impact recycling initiatives:

- Nestlé's "recycling stations" in Indonesia collect a fraction of their packaging waste, often without clear plans for proper processing.

- In India, Unilever's "Waste-Free World" campaign touts its collection of plastic waste, but investigative reporting revealed that much of this waste ends up incinerated, contributing to air pollution in low-income communities.

- Coca-Cola's partnership with The Ocean Cleanup involved funding a project to remove floating waste from rivers like the Citarum in Indonesia. But this was widely criticized as a distraction from their role in producing that waste in the first place.

These campaigns are designed not to fix the problem, but to reframe it. They transform massive structural issues into stories of personal responsibility and corporate benevolence.

The EU's Partial Reckoning

In Europe, tighter regulations have started to push back against this model, but even there, corporations resist.

The EU's 2019 Single-Use Plastics Directive aims to reduce items like plastic cutlery, straws, and stirrers. It also introduced Extended Producer Responsibility (EPR) schemes, making companies financially accountable for the waste they produce.

Faced with these rules, many corporations scrambled to find "sustainable" alternatives, which often turned out to be paper products coated with plastic, or biodegradable plastics that don't break down in real-world conditions. The EU later clarified that many of these substitutes still counted as single-use plastics, exposing the corporate tendency to game the system rather than comply with its intent.

Even with laws in place, enforcement remains patchy. Lobbying continues behind the scenes. And companies often shift their most polluting packaging to markets with weaker regulations, especially in Africa, Southeast Asia, and Latin America.

U.S. Case Study: The Battle Over Bottle Bills

In the U.S., attempts to introduce deposit-return systems (commonly known as "bottle bills") have been met with fierce resistance from beverage companies.

States like Oregon, Michigan, and California have shown that deposit systems significantly increase recycling rates, often doubling or tripling them. Yet when New York, Massachusetts, and Washington proposed similar systems, lobbying from Coca-Cola, PepsiCo, and the American Beverage Association killed or watered down the proposals.

Why? Because these systems put the cost and responsibility back on producers. They challenge the model of cheap, disposable packaging by making waste recovery part of the business model, rather than an afterthought left to taxpayers.

Plastic Offsets: A New Era of Greenwashing

As public scrutiny increases, some corporations have turned to plastic offsetting — a new form of greenwashing.

The logic is simple: for every tonne of plastic they produce, companies claim to "offset" it by funding cleanup projects elsewhere. But these schemes — often based in countries like the Philippines, Vietnam, or India — are fraught with problems:

- They rely heavily on informal labourers, often working in unsafe, exploitative conditions.

- They rarely address the plastic produced in the first place, focusing instead on cleanup after the fact.

- They create a market where plastic pollution becomes a tradable asset, rather than a problem to be solved.

It's carbon offsetting all over again — a feel-good mechanism that allows pollution to continue under a veneer of environmental responsibility.

The Real Fix: Production Reduction

There is no path to solving plastic pollution that doesn't involve making and using less plastic. But that's the one solution corporations won't touch — because it threatens their profit margins.

Instead, they double down on recyclability, circular economy rhetoric, and consumer blame. As long as they can keep the public believing that recycling is working — or could work "if only we tried harder" — they can delay the inevitable reckoning.

Governments in the Game

Governments — particularly in the Global North — have long been complicit in the myth of recycling. Not necessarily out of malice, but because it's politically convenient. Recycling offers a low-cost, high-visibility way to demonstrate concern for the environment without confronting the real culprits: unchecked production, industrial lobbying, and the consumer economy itself.

Instead of regulating plastic at the source or redesigning supply chains, governments have leaned on symbolic actions:

- Adding more bins

- Launching glossy recycling campaigns

- Announcing ambitious (but vague) "zero waste" goals

This creates the illusion of environmental progress — what scholars call "policy theatre." It soothes public concern and buys time. But crucially, it avoids the hard decisions that threaten powerful interests.

The Politics of Inaction

In democratic societies, few politicians want to stand

up and declare:

> "Recycling doesn't work. We need to ban half the packaging on supermarket shelves."

> It's a career-ending message. Voters might panic. Corporations definitely will.

So instead, policymakers embrace a safer strategy: double down on recycling. They promise to "improve systems," "educate the public," and "partner with industry." But the structural problem — the relentless production of non-recyclable plastic — is left untouched.

As a result, countries spend billions creating circular messaging rather than circular economies.

Case Study: The United Kingdom

The UK has long promoted itself as a recycling leader. But a 2021 Greenpeace investigation found that over half of the UK's plastic waste is exported — much of it ending up in Turkey and Malaysia, where it's illegally dumped or burned.

Despite this, the UK government continues to highlight recycling as a success story, citing percentage increases in collection rates while ignoring the fate of that collected waste. When pressure mounts, the government responds with consultations and pilot programs, not production cuts or bans on problematic plastics.

Attempts to legislate extended producer responsibility (EPR) — which would shift cleanup costs onto manufacturers — have been repeatedly delayed under industry pressure.

Case Study: United States — Local Recycling Collapse

In the U.S., the recycling crisis of 2018, following China's National Sword policy (which banned most foreign plastic waste), exposed the fragility of America's recycling system.

Cities from Philadelphia to Memphis began sending recyclables straight to landfills or incinerators. Some towns cancelled recycling altogether. The federal government, rather than stepping in with aggressive regulation or funding shifts, largely stayed silent.

Instead of launching a national rethink, states responded with media campaigns urging residents to "recycle right," blaming contamination and consumer behaviour rather than an unworkable economic model.

Case Study: Canada — Exporting the Problem

Canada, too, has claimed environmental leadership. But in 2019, a diplomatic spat with the Philippines revealed that over 100 containers of mislabeled Canadian waste had been shipped overseas, including soiled diapers and other unrecyclables disguised as plastic for recycling.

The incident embarrassed the Canadian government but failed to spark systemic change. Plastic bans have been slow and partial. Federal initiatives still heavily lean on consumer sorting and provincial recycling upgrades, despite clear evidence that most post-consumer plastic is landfilled or incinerated.

The Global South: Both Victim and Scapegoat

While Global North governments prop up the recycling myth to avoid political confrontation, the Global South often bears the brunt of its failure.

Countries like Indonesia, the Philippines, Vietnam, and Ghana have become dumping grounds for exported waste, often labelled as "recyclables." When this plastic ends up polluting rivers, oceans, or communities, Western governments and media often shift the blame to local mismanagement or "lack of infrastructure."

This framing allows Global North policymakers to deflect criticism while continuing business as usual at home.

When Governments Try — and Industry Pushes Back

Not all governments have been passive. Some have attempted stronger regulation, but the backlash is swift.

- In France, the government moved to ban plastic packaging on most fruits and vegetables by 2022. Supermarkets and trade groups lobbied hard, citing "economic hardship," and delayed the rollout.

- Kenya's 2017 ban on plastic bags was one of the toughest in the world. The plastics industry, backed by U.S. trade groups, lobbied to reverse it and prevent broader East African regulation. The ban survived, but not without political strain and attempts to weaken enforcement.

- In California, repeated attempts to implement producer responsibility laws have been met with lawsuits and aggressive lobbying by the American Chemistry Council and packaging lobbyists.

Even when a law is passed, enforcement is often underfunded, delayed, or quietly deprioritized.

Recycling as a Political Diversion

Ultimately, recycling has become a political shield:

- It delays structural reform

- It appeases environmentally conscious voters

- It deflects blame onto individuals and communities

- And it protects corporations from deeper scrutiny

By clinging to the myth, governments avoid admitting a hard truth: that solving plastic pollution requires less consumption, fewer products, and tighter controls — none of which are popular in a global economy fuelled by endless growth.

Why the Myth Persists

The recycling myth persists because it is useful. Not effective — *useful*. It's the rare illusion that works for nearly everyone involved in the system:

- Corporations use it as a public relations shield.

- Governments use it to show progress without confrontation.

- Consumers use it to soothe their conscience in an unsustainable world.

This convergence of interests has created a powerful *consensus of convenience* — one that prevents us from facing the more difficult truth: we are producing and consuming more than the Earth can handle.

Corporate Convenience

The myth allows corporations to continue business as usual while appearing to be environmentally responsible. With a well-placed "recyclable" label or a sustainability report boasting improved "recovery rates," they satisfy both regulators and consumers, without having to change their profit models.

Example:

- Coca-Cola, the world's top plastic polluter for several years running, continues to push single-use bottles while marketing itself as a "leader in sustainable packaging" through global recycling partnerships. In reality, less than 10% of its plastic ever gets recycled.

- Nestlé publicly commits to recyclability, but most of its multilayer sachets in Asia, especially in places like India and the Philippines, are non-recyclable, and the cost to recover and process them far exceeds their value.

Political Utility

Governments around the world lean on recycling because it buys time. Faced with intense industry lobbying and short political cycles, many officials prefer recycling initiatives over systemic legislation like production caps or consumption taxes.

Recycling offers a *non-threatening* form of environmental action:

- It doesn't challenge economic growth.

- It doesn't require a lifestyle change.

- It frames pollution as a downstream problem — one that can be solved by managing waste, not by reducing production.

It's policy theatre — and it plays well.

Even progressive governments often stick with recycling because the alternatives (such as zero-waste mandates or aggressive bans on petrochemical expansion) invite backlash from industry and voters alike.

Individual Morality

For individuals, recycling offers something deeper than utility: it offers absolution.

It allows us to continue participating in a hyper-consumerist system while believing we are doing our part. That belief is comforting — even sacred. It gives us agency in a world that often feels environmentally hopeless.

Psychologically, this is powerful:

- Throwing a bottle in the right bin *feels* like a moral act.

- Sorting waste becomes a daily ritual of redemption.

- Not recycling — even when we know the system is broken — *feels* wrong.

This is why even those who understand recycling's limits often continue doing it. Not because it works, but because we've been taught that it's virtuous.

The Fear of Admitting We Were Wrong

To abandon the myth of recycling is to confront an uncomfortable reality: that much of what we've done in the name of environmentalism has been performative or misguided. That our good intentions were *manipulated*. That decades of public messaging, school education, corporate campaigns, and government programs were not just insufficient — they were a strategic distraction.

This level of cognitive dissonance is hard to process.

For educators, environmentalists, politicians, and consumers alike, it raises painful questions:

- Were we complicit in a lie?

- Have we wasted decades on a false solution?

- If not recycling... then what?

That uncertainty creates resistance. It's easier to double down on the myth than to dismantle it and start over.

The Alternative Is Harder — But Necessary

Real solutions exist. But they are economically disruptive, politically risky, and culturally demanding:

- Reducing production means confronting the fossil fuel and plastics industries head-on.

- Investing in reuse means redesigning infrastructure, distribution, and habits.

- Accountability for polluters means changing laws, naming names, and breaking entrenched alliances.

These changes threaten powerful interests — and ask more of all of us. That's why they've been delayed. But they are the only path forward.

Because every year we waste defending a broken recycling system is a year we lose in the race to reverse ecological collapse.

Breaking the Spell

The myth of recycling persists because it's convenient — for everyone. But convenience is killing the planet.

To break the spell, we must be willing to:

- Name the lie.

- Confront the interests behind it.

- Rebuild a system that doesn't rely on illusions.

Recycling, in its current form, is not the solution. It's the distraction.

And the longer we cling to it, the longer we postpone the work that truly matters.

For decades, recycling has served as the cornerstone of modern environmentalism — a tidy, reassuring ritual in an otherwise messy world. But as we've seen, this ritual was never about solving the problem. It was about managing perception.

The myth of recycling was engineered by industries eager to deflect blame, embraced by governments keen to show progress without friction, and adopted by individuals looking for a sense of agency. It was the perfect solution for a world not yet ready to confront the real one.

But the planet is running out of time for illusions. We now know that the vast majority of plastic ever produced still exists — buried in landfills, floating in oceans, burned in incinerators, or breaking down into toxic micro-particles. We know that only a tiny fraction is ever truly recycled. And we know that as long as we allow recycling to masquerade as a solution, we give cover to those who profit from unchecked waste.

The first step toward real change is *letting go*. Letting go of the bedtime story. Letting go of the idea that individual gestures can undo systemic harm. Letting go of the hope that complex problems can be solved with convenient myths.

This doesn't mean surrender. It means clarity.

Only when we see the recycling myth for what it is — a story designed to pacify, not to protect — can we begin the hard but honest work of creating systems that truly align with sustainability, equity, and resilience.

Real solutions won't fit neatly in a bin.

But they might just give us a fighting chance.

A Simple Solution That Works

When Simple Is Revolutionary

We've been conditioned to believe that solving the plastic crisis must be complex: billion-dollar chemical plants, machine-learning robots, transnational policies, and timeframes stretching decades into the future. Solutions that are simple, local, or low-cost? They're often dismissed as unsophisticated — even when they work.

But history tells us something different.

Long before the rise of the consumer economy, reuse and repurposing were the default modes of human life. In pre-industrial societies across the globe, from rural India to the Andean highlands, tools, containers, and textiles were used until they fell apart, then transformed into something else. Waste was a luxury few could afford. Upcycling wasn't a buzzword. It was survival.

Then came the post-World War II boom: disposable packaging, global shipping, synthetic materials, and the mass production of plastics. Suddenly, waste became normalized — even aspirational. Plastics were cheap, durable, and convenient. But with that convenience came a problem we're still unable to manage.

By the 1980s, Western countries were generating more plastic than they could process. Recycling was promoted as the answer, but it was largely a myth in motion. According to a 2022 report by the OECD, of the 460 million tonnes of plastic produced globally each year, only 9% is recycled. The rest is burned, buried, or dumped — often in countries that didn't produce it.

In the United States, the numbers are even more stark. A comprehensive report from Greenpeace in 2022 found that only 5–6% of plastic waste is actually recycled. Most plastic labelled "recyclable" — especially films, wrappers, and multi-layered packaging — is not accepted by most facilities. Worse, even when it is collected, it often ends up incinerated or exported.

Meanwhile, advanced "chemical recycling" technologies — hyped as the future — remain stuck in pilot phases or fail to scale. The U.S. Environmental Protection Agency (EPA) acknowledges that these methods are "energy intensive, costly, and limited in the types of plastics they can process." Despite billions in public and private investment, few of these systems have produced meaningful results.

This is where upcycling becomes quietly

revolutionary.

Unlike recycling, which tries to break plastic down, upcycling works with plastic in its current form — no exotic tech, no high energy use, and no dependence on perfect sorting systems. It draws from the same principles that guided traditional societies: respect for material, frugality, and function. But it applies those values using modern tools: heat presses, moulds, shredders, and community-driven workshops.

Case in point:

- In India, grassroots groups like TrashCon and ReMaterials are creating affordable roofing from multi-layered plastic waste.

- In Indonesia, organizations like EcoBali are turning difficult-to-recycle plastics into bricks and panels for use in construction.

- In Nigeria, upcycling collectives use discarded sachets (plastic pouches for water and shampoo) to make furniture, insulation panels, and school benches.

- In Kenya, Gjenge Makers transforms plastic waste into highly durable paving bricks — five times stronger than concrete — using only a press and heat.

These efforts don't rely on government subsidies or elaborate regulatory frameworks. They operate in informal economies, solve real problems, and do so at a fraction of the cost of conventional recycling infrastructure.

The takeaway is simple but powerful:
Upcycling doesn't require permission, perfection, or policy alignment. It just requires intent and access to waste — something we have in abundance.

And in a world where the most expensive solutions are also the least effective, this kind of simple, decentralized intervention starts to look not just pragmatic, but revolutionary.

What It Looks Like in Practice

At its core, the upcycling model is elegantly straightforward. It doesn't rely on massive factories, robotic sorters, or chemical solvents. It works with what we already have — waste plastic, human labour, and low-tech tools — to create value from what was previously considered valueless.

Step-by-Step: How It Works

1. Collection
   The process begins with the collection of low-value plastic waste — the kind most

formal recyclers reject: chip bags, shopping bags, multilayer pouches, food wrappers, sachets, and films. This material, often labelled #4, #5, or unmarked, is nearly impossible to recycle through conventional systems.

2. Cleaning & Sorting
Plastics are washed, air-dried, and sorted manually. Since these materials often come from mixed waste streams, cleanliness is essential to ensure quality in the final product.

3. Shredding
The plastics are then fed through a mechanical shredder, often built from open-source blueprints or locally fabricated parts. This reduces them to confetti-like flakes that are easier to melt and mould.

4. Moulding or Extrusion
Shredded plastic is heated and pressed into moulds — or pushed through extrusion machines — to form solid items:

   o Bricks & pavers for roads, walkways, and flood control.

   o Roofing tiles for homes and schools.

- Fencing posts, outdoor benches, and construction panels.

- Modular furniture, public infrastructure (like bus stops or bike racks), or parts for low-income housing.

Some systems use injection moulds to create uniform shapes; others use compression moulding with heated plates or simple ovens. The tech stack is flexible and modular.

5. Deployment & Use
The final products are strong, weather-resistant, and low-cost. In many cases, they outperform traditional materials in durability, price, and resilience to moisture or decay.

Global Case Studies: Upcycling in Action

Kenya – Gjenge Makers Ltd.

Founded by Nzambi Matee in Nairobi, Gjenge Makers turns plastic waste into bricks five times stronger than concrete. They process up to 500–1000 kg of waste plastic daily, turning it into bricks used for sidewalks, schools, and local construction.

Their model:

- Uses local labour and handmade moulds.

- Employs young people and women from informal settlements.

- Produces bricks in vibrant colours and at a cost 40% cheaper than cement alternatives.

India – ReMaterials & TrashCon

- ReMaterials produces ModRoof, a modular roofing system made from upcycled packaging waste. It's lightweight, waterproof, and cools interiors — ideal for informal settlements and schools.

- TrashCon, based in Bengaluru, operates a fully closed-loop system that separates mixed waste, shreds plastics, and forms durable panels for infrastructure, all using proprietary machines that can run off-grid.

Indonesia – EcoBali & Rumah Plastik

These projects upcycle flexible plastic waste into tiles, panels, and furniture. Some operate out of modified shipping containers powered by solar panels. Local school programs encourage students to bring waste from home, linking waste reduction with educational outreach.

Philippines – The Plastic Flamingo ("The Plaf")

This social enterprise collects plastic waste from Manila's overflowing waterways and converts it into emergency shelter panels and construction boards. Much of their machinery is open-source and mobile, allowing deployment to disaster-prone areas.

Colombia – Conceptos Plásticos

By fusing plastic with rubber, this project produces LEGO-style bricks that snap together to build homes. A standard 40 m² house uses ~4 tons of plastic and can be assembled in under a week. The houses are fireproof, affordable, and earthquake-resistant.

Designed for Replication and Resilience

What sets this model apart is its scalability through simplicity. These systems:

- Can be set up for under $10,000 in many regions.

- Run with minimal energy input — some are fully solar.

- Operate independently of the national recycling infrastructure.

- Provide livelihoods to waste pickers, youth, and women.

Because they don't require industrial sorting or rare input materials, they're more resilient than traditional recycling systems, especially in countries where waste management is informal or underfunded.

And unlike conventional recycling, which often exports its footprint to the Global South, these solutions process waste at the source, closing the loop locally.

The Bigger Picture

This isn't fantasy or niche. It's already happening — in over 60 countries. What's missing is visibility, funding, and the policy support that entrenched recycling enjoys. With modest investment and knowledge-sharing, this model could be scaled globally, creating jobs, reducing landfill pressure, and cutting plastic pollution at the knees.

Why It's Scalable, Affordable, and Clean?

One of the greatest misconceptions about tackling the plastic crisis is that it requires massive industrial investment and sweeping government reform. That belief has led to decades of inertia. The upcycling model turns that idea on its head by proving that localized, low-tech solutions can be deployed affordably and immediately, with environmental, economic, and social impact.

Here's why this works:

Scalability Through Simplicity

Most traditional recycling systems are scale-dependent. They only become efficient when handling thousands of tons of sorted, uniform material. That's why they struggle in rural areas or developing economies: the infrastructure needed to sustain them simply doesn't exist.

Upcycling flips this logic.

- It doesn't require uniform material — even mixed, flexible plastics can be used.

- Machines are often locally fabricated or based on open-source blueprints (like Precious Plastic).

- Workshops can be run in shipping containers, garages, or under tents.

- It works in cities, towns, and villages alike — not just where recycling plants exist.

Because each unit operates independently, the system scales horizontally, not vertically. 10 communities running 10 small upcycling stations is just as effective — and more resilient — than one centralized factory.

> Case in point: In South Africa, community-run waste hubs in Johannesburg and Durban have upcycled over 20 tonnes of plastic each using just three machines and minimal electricity. Each site serves as both a production hub and an educational center.

Affordable by Design

Capital investment is low. A complete setup — shredder, extruder, moulds, and a heat source — can cost as little as $5,000 to $15,000, depending on configuration. Some setups run entirely off solar power, dramatically reducing operational costs.

Labour is local and inclusive. Upcycling centers:

- Employ waste pickers and provide them with safer, better-paid jobs.

- Engage youth and women in production, training, and design.

- Build ownership within the community, reducing reliance on foreign aid or government subsidies.

Material input is free — or nearly so. Most feedstock is waste plastic that no one else wants. Upcycling turns it into something sellable:

- A plastic brick can sell for $0.50 to $1.00, costing just $0.10 to produce.

- Tiles and roofing sheets undercut conventional options while lasting longer.

- School furniture made from plastic waste can be 40% cheaper than wooden alternatives and requires no maintenance.

  India's TrashCon operates small-footprint plastic panel units in schools and rural clinics that pay for themselves in under 12 months.

Environmentally Cleaner Than Recycling

Recycling is energy-hungry. It involves:

- Sorting and washing with industrial-scale water use

- High-temperature melting or chemical processes

- Large-scale transport to central facilities — often powered by fossil fuels

Upcycling, by contrast:

- Uses minimal water, often reused between batches

- In many cases, requires lower temperatures and less energy

- Is typically powered by renewable energy or basic electricity

- Keeps processing local, reducing transport emissions

In addition, upcycling avoids downcycling, where plastic gets turned into lower-quality materials until it's no longer usable. Instead, it turns waste into durable, long-term products with 10-30 year lifespans.

In Ghana, one NGO-led project used plastic bricks to build a school with zero concrete, reducing carbon emissions by 60% over conventional construction.

Built for Climate Adaptation

In climate-vulnerable regions, upcycled materials offer resilience:

- Bricks resist flooding and do not degrade in heat.

- Panels made from multilayer plastics act as insulation in homes.

- Upcycled construction is earthquake-resistant, lightweight, and durable.

And because materials don't rot, rust, or need paint, long-term maintenance is close to zero, making them ideal for infrastructure in the Global South or remote areas.

Social and Economic Co-Benefits

Upcycling isn't just environmental — it's transformative for communities.

- Creates local economies out of waste

- Provides skills training in mechanics, design, and entrepreneurship

- Builds community pride and ownership over waste solutions

- Helps normalize circular thinking in places often ignored by mainstream green policies

In Nigeria, youth-led microfactories are using plastic waste to produce school desks for rural districts. In doing so, they've cut absenteeism by 30%, created local jobs, and provided a model for circular development that doesn't depend on charity.

The upcycling model proves that the problem of plastic waste doesn't need to wait for billion-dollar solutions. With modest investment and community participation, waste becomes opportunity, and pollution becomes progress.

It's time we stopped waiting for someone else to fix the system. Upcycling is the system we've been waiting for — and it's already working.

The Barriers Are Political, Not Technical

If upcycling is so effective — low-cost, scalable, environmentally sound — then a fair question arises: why isn't this everywhere?

The answer is simple, though uncomfortable: because

it doesn't serve the interests of the current system.

A Decentralized Threat to Centralized Power

Upcycling challenges the established model of waste management, which is centralized, contractor-driven, and capital-heavy. Most public funding for waste infrastructure flows into:

- large-scale incinerators

- single-stream recycling plants

- landfill expansions

- public-private partnerships with multinational firms

Upcycling doesn't require any of that. It is:

- Decentralized: Can be community-run, off-grid, or mobile.

- Low-tech: Doesn't need proprietary systems or consultants.

- Empowering: Shifts control from municipalities and corporations to citizens.

That's not attractive to governments conditioned to

think in terms of contracts, not outcomes — or to officials trained to measure "progress" in GDP-linked procurement, not waste reduction.

> In Indonesia, several community-led plastic brick projects in Java were repeatedly denied permits and support, despite their proven success, simply because they didn't align with Jakarta's waste contractors' master plans.

The Corporate Conflict of Interest

For industries reliant on virgin plastic production — petrochemical companies, packaging manufacturers, FMCGs (fast-moving consumer goods) — the upcycling model is deeply inconvenient. Why?

Because it de-links waste from consumption. It shows that:

- Not all plastic is "recycled back into packaging."

- Communities can create value without buying more.

This undercuts the narrative that we can simply "recycle our way" out of the crisis — a story many corporations spend millions to sustain.

In the U.S., lobbying groups like the American

Chemistry Council have consistently fought against extended producer responsibility (EPR) laws, and they have never supported upcycling models in federal proposals, because they reduce the demand for new plastic inputs.

Recycling Industry as Gatekeeper

It may sound counterintuitive, but the traditional recycling industry also plays a part in blocking innovation.

Many waste management companies:

- Profit from collection and sorting contracts, not material recovery.

- Invested heavily in infrastructure that assumes linear flows — trucks, MRFs (Materials Recovery Facilities), export pipelines.

- View alternatives like upcycling as unregulated, unpredictable, and risky — even if they're effective.

There's an economic logic at work: a system that profits from inefficiency will resist efficiency.

In Kenya, when community upcyclers in Mombasa sought partnerships with municipal waste collectors, they were ignored — until international donors stepped in to fund a pilot. Only then did the city engage.

Regulatory and Legal Hurdles

In many countries, regulations are written for traditional waste processing, not for agile, small-scale models. As a result:

- Upcycling centres struggle to get licenses or zoning permits

- Standards are geared toward export or landfill

- There is little funding for informal or community systems

Even when policymakers want to support innovation, they are often bound by legacy frameworks that require years to revise.

> In the European Union, the Waste Framework Directive has strict classifications for "end-of-waste" criteria — meaning that even if a plastic panel is safe and durable, it may not be legally marketable until it meets certification that's too expensive for small players.

The Opportunity We're Ignoring

Despite all this, upcycling keeps working — often in the margins, often without support.

What's tragic is that this isn't some far-fetched idea waiting for tech breakthroughs. It's here. It's happening. It's just being ignored.

What stands in the way is not engineering, cost, or capacity.

It's politics.

It's fear of disruption.

It's a system that would rather protect wasteful models than empower people with working solutions.

As the director of one community upcycling cooperative in the Philippines put it:
"We're not waiting for permission to clean up our community. We're just doing it. But it's time the system stopped working against us."

The upcycling model is not a silver bullet, but it's a ready tool in a world desperate for real solutions. The only thing standing between where we are and where we could be is the willingness to shift power and redefine progress.

If we truly want to build a circular economy, we have to stop gatekeeping innovation and start scaling what already works.

A Path Forward

Let's be clear: Upcycling is not a silver bullet. It won't end the plastic crisis overnight. But unlike most of the narratives we've clung to — recycling myths, greenwashing pledges, policy promises without teeth — this model actually works. It works now, and it works in two critical ways:

Cleaning What's Already Out There

First, it tackles the mountain of plastic we've already discarded — the wrappers, sachets, bags, and multilayered junk clogging landfills, drains, and coastlines. By collecting and converting these hard-to-recycle plastics into long-lasting products, like construction blocks, roofing panels, furniture, and tiles, upcycling gives waste a second life.

No massive refineries. No advanced chemical processes. Just simple, replicable tools and community-based teams turning yesterday's garbage into tomorrow's infrastructure.

Stopping Waste Before It Spreads

But just as crucially, upcycling prevents waste before it becomes pollution.

Unlike traditional recycling systems that wait for plastics to flow through cities, rivers, and oceans before attempting recovery, upcycling programs can start at the point of consumption. Households, vendors, and small businesses can sort and contribute plastic waste directly to upcycling hubs — many of which are locally operated and deeply embedded in the community.

This community-first model not only increases recovery rates but also creates awareness, responsibility, and ownership. Residents stop seeing plastic as "someone else's problem" and start treating it as a resource they can actively manage — and benefit from.

The Impact: Measurable, Transformational

A well-implemented upcycling program — scaled across neighbourhoods, cities, and regions — could reduce plastic waste by up to 90% within a decade. Not through futuristic innovation, but through decentralized, real-world action. And if adopted globally with more aggressive coordination, entire ecosystems — including heavily polluted rivers and coastal areas — could begin to recover within 25 years.

That's a quarter-century to reverse a century of damage. It's bold. But it's doable.

From Trash to Transformation

We've spent decades treating plastic as either a disposable convenience or an impossible curse. What if we saw it instead as a building block, not just physically, but economically and socially?

- What if low-grade plastic became the raw material for jobs, local enterprises, and affordable housing?

- What if waste management became an engine for climate resilience rather than just a municipal headache?

- What if solving environmental problems didn't require guilt, complexity, or billion-dollar budgets, but simply a shift in who's empowered to act?

Upcycling Is a Tool — Not a Trend

This isn't about idealism. It's about realism. Upcycling doesn't pretend to solve everything, but it proves that we can solve something. Today. At scale. With the people and resources we already have.

It's a tool that deserves attention, investment, and integration into national and municipal waste strategies — especially in countries drowning in plastic and starved for infrastructure.

And most of all, it deserves to be owned by the communities who need it most, not controlled by consultants or corporations.

A Better Kind of Future

Recycling taught us to feel good. Upcycling invites us to do good — together.

It shows us that the solution to the plastic crisis may not be found in boardrooms or summits, but in workshops, rooftops, and hands-on collaboration. That's not a myth. That's a movement in the making.

And it's already begun.

What Is Upcycling?

Let's Get One Thing Straight

Upcycling is Not Arts and Crafts

Forget the Pinterest propaganda. This isn't about quirky flowerpots or "funky" lamp shades made from old Coke bottles. That's decoration. This is warfare against pollution, scarcity, and economic exclusion.

Upcycling is industrial survival.

It's taking plastic that was meant to rot in a ditch for 400 years and turning it into *infrastructure*.

Not conversation pieces. Not decor.

Assets. Tools. Shelter. Safety.

What Are We Really Talking About?

This is about turning used plastic into:

- **Construction Bricks**
  Made from high-density polyethylene (HDPE), shredded and pressed into interlocking forms that outperform clay or concrete in moisture resistance.

- **Roofing Tiles**
  Durable, heat-resistant, and far cheaper than traditional options. Perfect for flood-prone, storm-prone, or low-income areas.
- **Wall Panels**
  Compressed plastic sheets that insulate, resist termites, don't mould, and are easy to clean — ideal for clinics, schools, and housing.
- **Paving Blocks**
  Mixed with sand or fibre, these bricks are strong enough for sidewalks and parking lots, with excellent drainage and zero erosion.
- **Public Furniture**
  Benches, picnic tables, and bus stop seating — all made from a blend of shredded plastic and mouldable filler. Tough, vandal-resistant, and long-lasting.
- **Fencing and Poles**
  Wood rots. Metal rusts. Plastic? It just sits there and takes it — rain, sun, salt, dogs, time. Perfect for farms, schools, and public parks.
- **Drainage Systems**
  Gutters, pipe covers, channel boards — moulded to size from plastic waste. Stronger than tin, cheaper than PVC, and never corrodes.

These aren't DIY passion projects. These are high-impact infrastructure materials made from the same garbage we've been spending billions to "dispose of."

Why Does This Matter?

Because plastic isn't *just* trash. It's one of the most versatile materials ever created by humans. The problem isn't the material — it's the *mindset*.

We designed plastic to last forever, then used it for items we toss in under five minutes.

That's like forging steel swords to cut birthday cake.

Stupid, wasteful, and deeply ironic.

So What Does Upcycling Actually Do?

- It reclaims value from what the system says is worthless.
- It replaces expensive, unsustainable building materials with something cheaper and often better.
- It skips the emissions-heavy recycling process and gives plastic a new purpose *without breaking it down chemically*.
- It creates jobs, not just collecting waste, but manufacturing with it.

In the right hands, a discarded detergent bottle becomes a school bench. A pile of packaging becomes a wall. A landfill becomes a warehouse.

So No, This Isn't About Yogurt Cups

This isn't:
"What cute thing can I make for my desk?"
This is:
"How do I stop buying bricks, wood, and steel — and make them out of the trash that's choking our rivers?"

That's what upcycling is.

It's not for aesthetics. It's not for Instagram. It's for people who are sick of waiting for solutions and are ready to build them with whatever the hell's already here.

The Core Idea: Plastic ≠ Trash

Let's kill the myth right now:

Plastic was never the enemy.

We just used it like morons.

We took one of the most durable, versatile, and valuable materials ever invented, and used it to make disposable forks and bags. Then we acted surprised when it didn't disappear.

Plastic is:

- Strong — It holds buildings together in modern construction.

- Lightweight – Cheaper to move, ship, build, and scale.
- Mouldable – Can be shaped into damn near anything.
- Water-resistant – Try drowning it. You can't.
- Rot-proof – Nature can't break it down for centuries.

So what did we do?

We turned it into single-use garbage. Stuff designed to outlive us but only be useful for 5 minutes.

That's not a plastic problem.

That's a human stupidity problem.

Upcycling Doesn't Apologize for Plastic

It owns it.

This isn't recycling — where we waste energy trying to melt plastic back into some crude oil Frankenstein sludge and hope it behaves like new. That game is expensive, dirty, and full of failure points.

Upcycling is simpler. Smarter. Harsher.

It says:

"Plastic is already strong. Already durable. Already shaped. Why not use that?"

Instead of breaking plastic *down*, we break it *open* — literally.

We shred it, press it, mould it, and turn it into things that should last 50 years. Because plastic was built to last. That's not a defect. That's a feature — if you actually use it like it was meant to be used.

This Isn't Greenwashing.

It's weaponized realism.

This model doesn't pretend plastic will magically vanish if we "recycle more." It confronts the truth:

Plastic is here. It's everywhere. And it's not going anywhere.

So upcycling asks:

"What if we stopped fighting plastic's permanence... and started designing for it?"

Benches. Tiles. Bricks. Poles.

That's plastic doing what it should have been doing all along — replacing materials that cost more, weigh more, and damage the planet more.

You want a sustainable future? Stop burying plastic and start building with it.

Know Your Enemy: The 7 Types of Plastic — and What You Can (Actually) Do With Them

Before you start melting stuff, let's make one thing clear: not all plastic is equal.

Some melt like butter. Some release toxic fumes. Some you can shape into bricks. Others are basically useless in upcycling.

If you're going to turn trash into infrastructure, you need to know which plastics are your allies — and which ones will ruin your machines and your lungs.

Here's the battlefield:

♲ #1 PET (Polyethylene Terephthalate)

Used in: Soda bottles, water bottles, food containers

Upcycling rating: **Not your friend.**

PET melts at a high temperature and releases nasty gases. It absorbs water and degrades fast. Industrial recyclers can handle it, but small-scale upcyclers? Avoid.

Save it for proper recycling streams or creative non-heat uses.

♲ #2 HDPE (High-Density Polyethylene)

Used in: Milk jugs, shampoo bottles, detergent containers

Upcycling rating: *Gold standard.*

Melts clean. Easy to mould. Incredibly strong. Great for bricks, tiles, benches, and more.

Colour variety's a bonus — melt a rainbow or sort for uniformity. This is the backbone of most DIY upcycling setups.

♻ #3 PVC (Polyvinyl Chloride)

Used in: Plumbing pipes, window frames, credit cards

Upcycling rating: *Toxic nightmare.*

Do. Not. Touch.

PVC releases hydrochloric acid and dioxins when heated. Unless you want to gas yourself like it's a WWI trench warfare, leave it out. Industrial systems *sometimes* handle it, but for small-scale? Straight to landfill or skip entirely.

♻ #4 LDPE (Low-Density Polyethylene)

Used in: Plastic bags, cling wrap, squeezable bottles

Upcycling rating: *Tricky but doable.*

It's soft and flexible, which makes it tough to shred and mould. But with the right press and temperature control, you *can* use it for products like boards and tiles.

Caution: it's a pain. Only use if you're low on HDPE or want to experiment.

♻ #5 PP (Polypropylene)

Used in: Bottle caps, food containers, straws, furniture

Upcycling rating: *Very useful.*

PP melts clean, holds shape well, and is super common. Mixes well with HDPE in many applications.

Also, you know those annoying plastic chairs you see everywhere? Mostly PP. If that stuff can survive ten years outdoors and four weddings, it can definitely be repurposed into construction materials.

♻ #6 PS (Polystyrene / Styrofoam)

Used in: Takeout containers, insulation, disposable cutlery

Upcycling rating: *Just say no.*

Flammable, fragile, and full of air. It melts unevenly, gives off toxic fumes, and produces weak, brittle products. Best used as insulation filler (if at all), but usually? Not worth the trouble.

♻ #7 Other / Mixed Plastics

Used in: Everything else — multilayer packs, electronics, weird blends

Upcycling rating: *Wild card.*

Too unpredictable. Some #7 plastics are fine; most are a Frankenstein mess of resins and adhesives that don't melt clean or mould right. Use with extreme caution, or better yet, avoid until you've mastered the basics.

The Sweet Spot for Upcycling

Focus your early builds on:

- HDPE (#2)

- PP (#5) Optional

- LDPE (#4) — once you've got your footing

And remember: Clean your plastics.

Dirt, food, oil, and labels mess with the bonding process and reduce final product quality. Upcycling isn't just melting trash — it's industrial design with garbage as your supply chain.

Sorting & Preparation: The Foundation of Every Good Build

Step 1: Sorting by Plastic Type

Think of this as separating wood from metal before building a house — you don't want garbage mixing with your bricks.

How to Sort:

- Look for the plastic codes: Most plastics have the triangle with a number (⚠ to ⚠).

- Use the float test (for advanced users):
    - Toss a small plastic piece into water.

    - HDPE and LDPE float.

    - PET, PVC, and others sink.

    - Not perfect, but a helpful extra check.

- Melt test: If you're unsure, heat a tiny sample and watch:
    - HDPE and PP melt smoothly.

○ PVC and PS release nasty fumes or bubble weirdly.

Tip: Keep labelled bins or sacks per type. Do this from Day 1. Mixing plastics creates structural weakness, like mixing cement with flour.

Step 2: Cleaning — No One Likes Filthy Plastic

Melted peanut butter, laundry detergent residue, and mouldy juice? Yeah — your shredder doesn't like that. Neither does your nose.

How to Clean:

- Rinse thoroughly — hose, bucket, or drum. Strip out all organic and sticky residues.

- Use soapy water if needed. Degreasing is key, especially with food containers.

- Scrub if stubborn — old dish brushes, car wash sponges, or mechanical washers work.

Goal: Clean enough to eat off it. (Not that you should. But still.)

Step 3: Label & Cap Removal — Small Details, Big Impact

Most plastic bottles and containers come with labels made of different plastics or paper, which can mess with bonding, melting, and end-product appearance.

How to Remove:

- Caps & Rings: Often made from PP (#5) and not the same as bottle plastic.
  - Twist or cut off caps and neck rings before shredding.

- Labels:
  - Adhesive paper: Soak in hot water, then peel.

  - Shrink wrap: Cut with a blade — it won't melt the same.

  - Printed ink: Fine to leave on (it'll discolour the plastic, but no performance issue).

- Glue residue? Scrape or use citrus-based solvents (sparingly).

Step 4: Drying — Moisture Is the Silent Killer

Even a few drops of water inside your shredded plastic can cause:

- Steam bubbles

- Cracks

- Weak structural integrity

- Popcorn-sounding explosions in machines

Drying Techniques:

- Air dry: Spread plastics out on mesh trays in the sun.

- Drying racks: DIY with old window screens or repurposed crates.

- Drum drying (advanced): If you're processing large volumes, use a rotating dryer with heated air.

Tip: Dry until it's *crispy*, not just damp-free. Moisture loves hiding inside folds and cracks.

Step 5: Shredding Prep — Size Matters

You can't melt or mould full-size jugs or detergent bottles. They need to be chopped into shredder-friendly sizes.

Pre-cutting tips:

- Use heavy-duty scissors, machetes, or saws to break large items into manageable chunks.

- Avoid metal parts (like handles or clips). One screw can wreck a shredder blade.

Summary Checklist (Print This on Your Wall):

- Sorted by type (HDPE, PP, etc.)
- All food/grease/sticky stuff removed
- Labels, caps, and rings are separated
- Thoroughly dried — no trapped water
- Pre-cut for shredder access

Prep is where most upcyclers fail.

But if you get this part right? Everything after — the melt, the mould, the build — becomes faster, smoother, and way more reliable.

Building a Full Upcycling System: Use Every Type of Plastic

Not all plastics behave the same. Some melt cleanly. Some release toxins. Some don't melt at all — but that doesn't mean they're useless.

So here's how to stop thinking of plastic as trash, and start thinking of it as a toolbox of materials, each with its own function:

Common Plastics and Their Best Uses

Type	Examples	Processing	Best Used For
HDPE (Type 2)	Milk jugs, detergent bottles	Low-temp melt (120–180°C)	Bricks, benches, panels
LDPE (Type 4)	Plastic bags, wrap	Very flexible, hard to shape alone	Roofing tiles, compression mould filler
PP (Type 5)	Food tubs, bottle caps	Good melt flow, durable	Structural bricks, panels, joints

PS (Type 6 - Styrofoam)	Foam packaging, trays	Dissolve in acetone (don't heat)	Glue, filler, coating, insulation
PET (Type 1)	Water/ soda bottles	High melt point, degrades	Fibre/fabric, not great for blocks
Mixed/ Unknown	Anything unmarked	Avoid high-temp melt	Shred for filler or dissolve for binder

The System at a Glance:

- HDPE & PP: Your main *building blocks* — bricks, panels, tiles.

- LDPE: Can be blended for flexibility or insulation. Great for roofing sheets.

- PS (Styrofoam): Don't melt — dissolve into glue to bind bricks or coat panels.

- PET: Not ideal for heating. Can be cut into fibres or used in non-load-bearing roles.

- Everything else? Filler, coating, adhesive, or a challenge for someone smarter.

Want to Dive Into Specific Builds?

Hell yes, you do. That's where the magic happens. The next section will walk you through step-by-step builds, starting with:

- Plastic Bricks: Strong, modular, scalable

- Benches & Furniture: Outdoor, public-use proof of concept

- Roofing Tiles: Lightweight and waterproof

- Wall Panels & Fencing: Durable alternatives to wood or sheet metal

- Using Styrofoam as Glue: Turning a problem into a binder

Ready to melt, mould, and make something real out of trash?

Let's build.

The Machines Are Already Here

You don't need a factory. You don't need millions. You don't even need permission.

You need four key ingredients — and a bit of stubbornness.

The Core Machines

1. Shredder
This is the heart of the system. It takes plastic waste and chews it into flakes.

- Think woodchipper, but for plastic.

- Outputs uniform shreds, perfect for melting or compressing.

- Can be hand-cranked, motorized, or solar-powered.

- Open-source versions use car parts, bike gears, and cheap steel.

2. Extruder
This machine takes the shreds and melts them into a continuous flow, like a giant 3D printer nozzle.

- Use it to create beams, planks, pipes, or mould filler.

- Ideal for linear products like fence posts or slats.

- Different nozzles = different shapes.

- It can be built from old heating elements, augers, and steel tubing.

3. Compression Mould (or Press)
Load plastic shreds into a mould and apply heat and pressure. Let it cool. Boom — you've got a brick.

- The most versatile tool in the kit.

- Great for making tiles, panels, bricks, and furniture parts.

- Can be manual (jack press), hydraulic, or electric.

- Moulds can be made from welded steel or cast aluminum.

4. Workspace
  Not a lab. Not a warehouse. Just space to operate safely.

- A garage, community hall, shipping container, or open-air shelter.

- Needs ventilation, surfaces, and some basic tools.

- Add storage for raw materials, moulds, and finished products.

What Makes This Revolutionary?

- Open-source plans (Precious Plastic, OpenMachines, YouTube engineers)

- Scrap-based builds (salvage yards are goldmines)

- Off-grid friendly (some setups run entirely on solar)

- Modular + scalable (start with one machine, expand as needed)

This isn't startup porn. This is real-world, low-cost industrial infrastructure designed for people without PhDs or venture capital.

It's Already Happening

- In Kenya, slums are building schools out of plastic bricks.

- In India, women's co-ops run presses in rural villages.

- In Brazil, plastic roofing tiles are replacing asbestos.

- In Indonesia, whole communities operate microfactories in recycled shipping containers.

This is manufacturing for the rest of us.

It's industrial power, unplugged from the grid — and the grip of red tape.

No more "somebody should."

You've got the machines. You just need to turn them on.

It's Ugly — But It Works

Let's not sugarcoat it.

You're not making showroom furniture. You're not impressing design blogs. This isn't Scandinavian minimalism.

You're making hard, heavy, functional things — with scars.

The bricks might be uneven. The tiles might have bubbles. The surface might look like it came out of a Mad Max garage.

So what?

This is not about aesthetics.

It's about resilience.

- You're building benches that won't splinter or rust in the rain.

- Tiles that keep families dry through monsoons.

- Bricks that don't crumble under heat, rot, or flood.

- Fencing that doesn't warp, corrode, or need paint every year.

You're not selling to trend-chasers. You're solving problems for people who need function, not fashion.

And the kicker? This crap was supposed to be buried. Or burned. Or floating off the coast of Puerto Rico.

Now it's holding up a roof. Supporting a wall. Lining a garden.

Form Follows Function

Ugly is honest.

Ugly is strong.

Ugly is useful.

That yogurt lid? It's now part of a drainage system.

That chip bag? A sliver in a school fence.

That cracked laundry basket? Reborn as the leg of a park bench.

If you want sleek edges and glossy polish, go talk to Apple.

If you want real-world survival infrastructure from garbage, you're in the right place.

Because when the storms hit, no one asks what colour the bricks are.

They just want to know: Will it hold?

And the answer is: Hell yes.

The Takeaway

If you thought upcycling was some quirky little eco-hipster side project, time to slap yourself awake.

This isn't about Mason jars and Pinterest hacks.

This is an industry born in the ashes.

This is infrastructure from garbage.

This is a parallel economy, built by people who got tired of waiting for policy and picked up a wrench instead.

You're not just keeping plastic out of the ocean.

You're pulling your community out of dependence, one ugly brick at a time.

You're not "going green."

You're going rogue.

This is the hard reset, not the polished version they pitch at climate conferences.

This is the dirt-under-your-nails, smoke-in-your-eyes, boots-on-the-ground version.

The one that starts in shipping containers, alleys, schoolyards, and ends with villages, towns, and cities building their way out of decay.

You're not recycling.

You're not protesting.

You're not raising awareness.

You're rebuilding — from the wreckage of a system that sold us convenience, then disappeared when the cleanup bill came due.

This isn't symbolic.

This is survival.

So no, it won't be pretty.

But it'll be yours.

It'll work.

And one day, they'll say:
   "This all started with one person who stopped waiting."

Welcome to the work.

Plastic as Currency

Trash Isn't Worthless. We Just Forgot How to Value It.

We've been trained — programmed, really, to see trash as the end of a thing. As failure. As something to hide, bury, or burn.

But that's a lie of convenience.

Trash is raw material. It's input. It's the start of a cycle, not the end of one.

And plastic? Plastic is the king of that forgotten kingdom.

Money is a social agreement. A myth we all agree to believe in. It only works because we trust it represents something useful.

Labour, on the other hand, is real. Sweat, skill, time, energy — those are the things that create value in the world.

So here's the uncomfortable truth:

- Plastic was made with labour.

- It was delivered with fuel, machines, and people.

- It was packaged, marketed, and consumed with the entire weight of the global economy.

Then we tossed it.

We threw away all that value just because we couldn't be bothered to look at it differently.

Plastic Is Everywhere — and It's Permanent.

That's not a weakness. That's an opportunity.

Plastic has everything you want in a currency or building material:

- It's lightweight.

- It's durable.

- It's mouldable.

- It doesn't rot.

- It doesn't disappear.

The same qualities that make plastic a nightmare for oceans make it a miracle for infrastructure if you have the guts to use it.

What If We Stopped Treating It Like a Liability...

Not "waste management."

Not "clean-up drives."

Not "corporate social responsibility."

What if we saw plastic as something to be banked, not buried?

Stored, not burned?

Traded, not trashed?

Because where others see risk, you can build leverage.

A kilo of plastic is a construction block waiting to happen.

A bag of wrappers is a paycheck in disguise.

A city's landfill is its next round of housing, fencing, pavement, and jobs.

...And Started Treating It Like Leverage?

This isn't charity. This isn't aesthetics.

This is economics — built from the ground up.

When you control the material that no one else wants, you become the one everyone needs.

This is about power.

Real, tangible, industrial power — forged from the literal bottom of the barrel.

The systems in charge won't teach you this.

But if you learn it?

You're dangerous.

Because you'll never look at trash the same way again.

The Currency of Scarcity

In many parts of the world, money is scarce, not because people aren't working, but because the economy was never designed to recognize their work. No bank accounts. No reliable income. No access to loans or formal employment. But one thing these communities have in abundance is plastic waste.

And that's the irony: what the world calls "waste" is often the most consistent and available resource people have.

Plastic is everywhere. It doesn't rot, it doesn't rust, and it doesn't go away. It's more permanent than most jobs. But we've been trained to see it as a nuisance, a byproduct, a problem to manage, not a material to build with.

What if we flipped that thinking?

Upcycled plastic can be transformed into durable goods — bricks, tiles, panels — the very materials needed for shelter, sanitation, and community infrastructure. A kilo of shredded plastic can make a construction brick. Ten bricks can build a wall. A few hundred bricks and you have a small classroom or shop. Multiply that, and you're talking about schools, clinics, and homes built from what was once clogging a gutter.

That means plastic isn't just potential — it's capital. Real value that just needs reshaping.

If a brick costs money, and plastic can be turned into a brick, then plastic is simply money that hasn't been minted yet. We're not talking about some utopian barter system. We're talking about a model where value is extracted from the one material we have too much of. Where plastic becomes a unit of trade — a means of production in a parallel economy.

And here's where it gets uncomfortable: the poorer the community, the richer they are in this untapped resource. Plastic is their inheritance — not by choice, but by design. Global supply chains dump it, and local systems don't know what to do with it. But instead of seeing plastic as a burden, we can treat it like leverage.

Of course, this kind of economy won't look like Wall Street. It won't involve hedge funds or venture capital. It'll involve garage-based workshops, homemade machines, and community-led builds. But that doesn't make it less real. It makes it more honest.

This isn't about eco-activism or charity. It's about utility. Use what you've got to get what you need. In a world of artificial scarcity, plastic is a real and ugly surplus — and that makes it powerful.

Treat it accordingly.

Trade Trash for Value

In places where cash is hard to come by, value doesn't disappear — it just shifts form. When formal economies fail to serve people, informal ones emerge. And in many parts of the world, plastic is already stepping in to fill the gap.

You don't need a stock market to create a value exchange. You need a swap station where plastic waste can be traded for things people need: food, education, medicine, and dignity.

In Indonesia, the "Waste Bank" model has proven this concept. Residents bring in bags of sorted plastic and receive credits toward food, transport vouchers, or school fees. In some towns, plastic isn't just trash —

it's tuition. In parts of Kenya, clinics accept plastic in exchange for discounted medical services. In India, children earn school supplies and meals by collecting bottles from the roadside. In the Philippines, entire neighbourhoods are now supported by plastic-to-pay programs, where the very waste polluting their streets becomes the raw material of survival.

This isn't about idealism. It's logistics. Plastic is abundant, durable, and easy to verify. One kilo weighs what it weighs. One bottle is one bottle. You don't need a central bank to set its price — you just need a system that gives it a use.

Instead of letting plastic sit in drains or rot in ditches (spoiler: it doesn't), it can be redirected into community value chains. It becomes food on the table, medicine at the clinic, a uniform on a child's back. Every plastic wrapper that would have otherwise been burned or buried suddenly becomes part of a new social contract: bring something in, get something out.

The trade-off isn't just economic, it's psychological. People stop being beggars and become participants. Kids stop skipping school and become collectors. Parents stop choosing between lunch and medicine and start earning both through effort. That shift, from dependency to contribution, is powerful. It restores agency where systems have taken it away.

The concept is not new. Barter systems have existed for centuries. But this is barter for the 21st century — using the one thing we've overproduced as the foundation for the things we've underdelivered.

And the best part? The infrastructure is minimal. A shed, a digital scale, a record book. That's it. The value doesn't come from the tech — it comes from the trust. If the community believes plastic has worth, then it does. And once that belief takes root, the possibilities multiply.

We're not just talking about recycling. We're talking about reinvention — of waste, of work, of what counts as "money."

Because in the end, value is what people agree it is. And if plastic can feed a child or pay a doctor, then it's already worth more than most currencies in circulation.

Rebuilding Trust Through Exchange

Something subtle but powerful happens when people see their trash being turned into something useful. It's not just about cleaner streets or fewer plastic bags in gutters — it's about a shift in the collective mindset. Where there was once apathy or frustration, there's now pride. Possibility. Ownership.

Communities that have long been neglected by government services or bypassed by economic development often carry an invisible weight: the feeling that nothing they do really matters. But when waste, something they've been told is worthless, is suddenly turned into bricks for classrooms or benches for bus stops, the equation flips. That plastic bag isn't just a nuisance anymore. It's a resource.

This transformation doesn't require speeches or policies. It happens through action. People show up with bags of sorted plastic not because they were told to, but because they've seen what it can become. They're not just cleaning up their streets — they're investing in them. They're not waiting for aid — they're contributing to a system that rewards their effort.

Trust begins to rebuild. Not because institutions delivered, but because the community delivered for itself.

Children begin to understand that even something as humble as a bottle cap can be part of building something bigger. Parents feel that their time spent collecting and sorting isn't just labour, it's value. Even the act of dropping off plastic at a swap station becomes a ritual of contribution: "I matter. What I bring has worth."

And something else happens: behaviour changes. When plastic becomes valuable, it's no longer thrown away so casually. Littering declines. Hoarding begins. Streets stay cleaner not because of fines or fear, but because the community now sees waste as an opportunity.

More importantly, this kind of local, practical exchange creates a system of trust in a place where institutional trust may be non-existent. People believe in what they can see. And when they see a wall built from yesterday's trash or groceries handed over in return for collected bottles, it rewires what they believe is possible.

You're not just cleaning up plastic. You're cleaning up the remnants of neglect. You're clearing space for agency and dignity to return.

This is how you build not just better streets, but stronger communities, where participation replaces dependency, and the smallest contributions are proof that everyone has something to offer.

Backed by Labour, Not Banks

The beauty of a plastic-based exchange system is its grounding in something that modern currencies often lack: tangible labour. This isn't about speculation. There are no bubbles to burst, no coins to mine, no servers burning energy in remote data centers. It's not crypto — it's commitment. It's not a promise backed by abstract confidence in an institution; it's value created by the hands of ordinary people doing visible, measurable work.

Every brick made from waste plastic carries a story. Someone bent down to pick it up off the street. Someone sorted it by type, cut off the labels, and cleaned it. Someone ran it through a shredder, poured it into a mould, and waited as it cooled into shape. That object — whether it ends up as a roofing tile, a wall panel, or a bench — is not theoretical. It exists because someone put in the hours to make it exist.

This is a kind of economy that doesn't rely on credit scores or startup funding. It runs on sweat equity. And unlike financial systems that can fail due to greed, corruption, or collapse, this one is self-sustaining. As long as people have plastic and are willing to work, value can be created. Even better, it stays in the community.

Contrast that with the global economy. So much of it is based on things most people never touch or fully understand: futures, derivatives, debt instruments. Money flows in and out of communities without ever taking root. But when a community member can trade a week's worth of sorted plastic for construction material, groceries, or school supplies, it's more honest than most of the currencies printed by central banks.

This is economic participation at its most inclusive. It doesn't require literacy, formal education, or digital access. It rewards effort directly. Everyone can join. Everyone can contribute. And the output — benches, bricks, shelters — has both immediate utility and long-term impact.

The value is real. And it's built by the people who need it most.

The Endgame: Closed-Loop Economies

What if the very thing polluting our streets could become the foundation of a new economy?

Picture this: in a small town or urban neighbourhood, plastic is no longer garbage. It's collected, weighed, and processed just steps from where it was thrown away. Local machines — often built from scrap — shred, melt, and mould that waste into bricks, benches, tiles, and other essentials. Every stage of the process employs someone: the collector, the sorter, the technician, the builder. And every product made stays in the community, as homes, schools, drainage, furniture, and fences.

This is the vision of a closed-loop economy, one

where materials never leave the system and value is constantly regenerated by the people who live there. No imports, no debt, no dependence on international supply chains or foreign aid. Just local labour transforming local waste into local wealth.

It's an economy powered by what others overlook: persistence, community trust, and trash. The plastic that once clogged rivers and killed livestock becomes the backbone of a new form of infrastructure. It doesn't just clean up the environment, it reshapes the economy.

These aren't abstract dreams. Pilot projects in countries like Colombia, Nigeria, and Indonesia are already proving that such systems can be built, scaled, and maintained without massive outside investment. They thrive on grit, open-source designs, and the willingness of communities to reimagine what's possible.

At its core, a closed-loop economy is about resilience. It makes people less vulnerable to economic shocks, supply chain disruptions, or shifting political winds. And by valuing the overlooked, plastic, labour, and local knowledge, it flips the script on scarcity.

What was once a curse becomes a catalyst.

This isn't just cleanup. It's a quiet revolution, one brick, one bench, one block at a time.

The New Exchange Rate

In the old world, value was defined by what you owned. Money in the bank. Degrees on the wall. Land, stocks, inheritance.

But in the communities left out of that equation — where jobs are scarce, banks don't lend, and formal systems don't serve — something else quietly accumulates: waste. Tons of it. Every week. Mostly plastic.

For decades, this plastic has been treated like a nuisance, or worse, a curse. But what if it's actually a resource? A raw material for industry. A token of labour. A unit of value.

Imagine a new exchange rate:

1 plastic bottle = 1 unit of power.

Not metaphorical power, but real, material power.

Power to build: Turn it into bricks, panels, or tiles.

Power to earn: Trade it for food, school fees, or healthcare.

Power to own: Use it to help build a home, start a business, or reshape a neighbourhood.

This isn't charity. It's not a handout wrapped in green branding.

This is about agency — the ability to act, to build, to contribute — using what you already have. It's about flipping the script on what counts as wealth. Because plastic doesn't degrade easily. It doesn't rust, rot, or evaporate. It lasts. That permanence, once a problem, now becomes a feature.

And the kicker? No one's coming to take it from you. It's too dirty for Wall Street. Too scattered for monopolies. Too decentralized for control.

That's the power of the new economy. It's loud. It's chaotic. It's grounded in labour, in community, in resourcefulness.

It's not the system's economy.

It's ours.

And it starts with one bottle.

Products That Prove the Point

Upcycling is only as powerful as the products it creates. It's one thing to talk about sustainability or circular economies — it's another to stand in front of a structure made entirely from what the world once called trash.

This chapter is not about theory. It's about proof.

Proof that plastic can be more than pollution.

Proof that waste can become wealth.

Proof that real, usable, durable infrastructure can emerge from the leftovers of consumerism.

These aren't abstract ideas or Pinterest projects. These are tested, replicable solutions, already being used in towns and cities across the Global South — in refugee camps, informal settlements, flood zones, rural schools, and inner-city neighbourhoods. They've been built by community members, local entrepreneurs, small cooperatives, and self-starters using open-source tools and everyday waste.

We're talking about bricks that build homes.

Roofing tiles that resist mould and rain.

Benches that survive storms.

Furniture that never rots.

Walkways that keep schoolyards dry.

This is the toolbox of belief, the chapter that silences the critics and empowers the doers.

Because here's the truth: people don't rally around ideas. They rally around results. You can convince someone with statistics, but you win them with a product they can sit on, sleep under, or walk across. That's when upcycling stops being a concept and becomes a movement.

In the pages ahead, we're going to explore a series of proven, scalable products made from upcycled plastic. We'll look at:

- How they're made

- What makes them effective

- Where they're already being used

- And most importantly, why they matter

Because every product you'll read about isn't just solving an environmental problem. It's solving a human one. A housing crisis. A lack of school infrastructure. The absence of public seating. Drainage in monsoon zones. Basic dignity in places where systems have failed.

These products are more than creative, they're infrastructural interventions. They create jobs. They spark trust. They prove that progress doesn't have to wait for policy. That communities can build their own future, with the very materials that were choking them yesterday.

So, whether you're a policymaker, builder, entrepreneur, or activist, this chapter is your reference manual. It's the collection of what works. And it's where ideas turn solid.

Let's get into it.

Plastic Bricks

In many parts of the world, building with traditional materials like concrete and clay is increasingly unsustainable, both financially and environmentally. Enter plastic bricks: a simple but revolutionary concept that transforms discarded plastic into strong, durable construction blocks. What began as small-scale experiments is now becoming mainstream in countries like Colombia, Nigeria, South Africa, and India, where innovation often grows out of necessity.

Plastic bricks are typically made by shredding collected plastic waste, mixing it with sand or fillers, and compressing it into moulds using simple machines. Some processes involve heat; others rely on cold compression techniques. But the result is the same: a solid, stackable brick with real-world structural integrity.

Why it works is rooted in both material science and context. Plastic bricks have excellent compressive strength, in many cases comparable to or exceeding standard cement blocks. They don't absorb water like porous bricks, which means they don't swell, crack, or erode in humid or flood-prone areas. And unlike wood, they're immune to rot and termites, making them particularly useful in tropical regions where both are constant threats.

From retaining walls in hilly slums to public toilets in rural villages, these bricks are being used to construct everything from homes and schools to drainage channels and boundary walls. Their modular design also allows for quick assembly, ideal for emergency housing or disaster response scenarios.

The cost savings are equally compelling. When made locally, with community-sourced waste and open-source machinery, plastic bricks can be 40–60% cheaper than traditional building materials.

That's not just a reduction in price, that's the difference between building or not building at all.

But the impact goes beyond just affordability. Every brick represents a chain of value, from the person who collected the plastic to the one who processed it, to the builder who laid it. What was once an informal and often exploitative labour sector (waste picking) becomes part of a formalized, regenerative industry.

The community value is twofold: shelter and employment. In neighbourhoods long neglected by public infrastructure, plastic bricks are offering a way to self-build, not just homes, but dignity. They also inject cash and purpose into local economies by turning waste into work. One ton of plastic, instead of polluting a riverbank, might build a family's house. Or a classroom. Or a clinic.

That's not just sustainable — that's transformative.

Modular Wall Panels

In regions where rapid construction is critical, whether for emergency shelters after disasters or to expand under-resourced schools, modular wall panels made from upcycled plastic are proving to be a game-changer. Countries like Kenya, Indonesia, and the Philippines have seen the successful adoption of these panels, showcasing how waste can be repurposed into practical building materials that meet real community needs.

These wall panels are typically made from shredded, pressed multilayer plastics, the kind that often cause the biggest headaches in recycling centers, such as snack wrappers, plastic bags, and other mixed plastics. By compressing these materials into flat, sturdy sheets, the panels are lightweight yet strong, offering a viable alternative to traditional wood or drywall.

Why these panels work lies in their combination of practicality and performance. Their lightweight means they can be installed quickly and with minimal labour, a crucial factor in emergency response or rapid development contexts. For communities rebuilding after floods, earthquakes, or other crises, speed is essential, and these panels deliver.

Another significant advantage is their insulating properties. Because plastics don't conduct heat well, the panels provide a natural barrier against the sun's heat in hot climates, helping maintain cooler indoor temperatures without the need for expensive air conditioning. This contributes directly to energy savings and increased comfort in environments where electricity access is limited.

From a cost perspective, plastic wall panels are highly competitive. Compared to conventional materials like plywood or drywall, they can be 30–50% cheaper, and thanks to their lightness, they reduce transportation and handling costs as well. Additionally, these panels are often 50–70% lighter, making logistics more efficient and environmentally friendly.

Beyond the numbers, the community benefits are profound. Using plastic panels reduces the demand for timber, which is a critical win against deforestation and environmental degradation in many parts of the world. Moreover, the panels can be manufactured in compact, container-based facilities, bringing production closer to where the waste and the need exist. This decentralized model empowers communities to manage their own building resources, creating jobs and fostering local economic resilience.

In places where infrastructure is lacking, modular plastic wall panels are not just construction materials; they are a step toward self-sufficiency, sustainability, and dignity. They turn what was once considered worthless waste into the very fabric of homes, schools, and businesses.

Roofing Tiles

In many vulnerable communities, the roof is the first line of defence against harsh weather, from pounding rains to scorching sun and fierce winds. Traditional roofing materials can be costly, heavy, or prone to deterioration, leaving many homes exposed and at risk. This is where upcycled plastic roofing tiles are making a real impact, with successful implementations in countries like Uganda, Ghana, and Haiti.

These roofing tiles are crafted by combining shredded plastic waste with other materials, such as sand or composite fillers, which are then pressed or moulded into sturdy, weatherproof tiles. Some innovative designs include interlocking features, allowing for faster, more secure installation without the need for nails or complex tools. This design simplicity makes roofing accessible even to communities with limited construction expertise.

Why these roofing tiles work can be summed up in their durability and resilience. Plastic is naturally resistant to moisture, mould, and rot, common problems that plague traditional roofing made from wood, metal, or organic materials. Unlike galvanized metal roofing, which can rust over time and amplify heat inside a home, plastic tiles do not corrode and have lower heat absorption, contributing to cooler indoor environments. This is a significant comfort and health benefit in hot climates.

From a cost perspective, plastic roofing tiles can be priced at up to half the cost of galvanized metal sheets, making them affordable for low-income households. This price advantage, combined with their durability, means that homeowners save money not only upfront but also over time due to lower maintenance and replacement needs.

The community value extends beyond just providing shelter. By offering an affordable, durable roofing solution, these tiles help upgrade informal settlements, many of which are located in flood-prone or storm-prone regions. Improved roofing reduces vulnerability to natural disasters, protecting lives and property. Moreover, producing these tiles locally creates jobs in plastic collection, processing, and manufacturing, injecting income into the community while tackling plastic pollution head-on.

In essence, plastic roofing tiles are not merely construction materials; they are a practical, scalable response to intersecting crises of housing insecurity, climate vulnerability, and waste management.

Paving Blocks and Tiles

Paving blocks and tiles may not sound glamorous, but their role in transforming public spaces and improving everyday life is profound. In countries like India, Tanzania, and Brazil, these functional upcycled plastic products are making their mark by revitalizing walkways, driveways, schoolyards, and bustling marketplaces.

What makes plastic paving blocks so effective is their strength and versatility. Engineered to handle the weight of foot traffic and even light vehicles, these blocks provide durable, long-lasting surfaces that are both practical and safe. Their non-slip texture adds an important safety element, especially in wet or high-traffic areas, reducing accidents and making communal spaces more accessible.

The manufacturing process typically involves mixing shredded plastic waste with sand or cement, creating composites that balance durability with cost-efficiency. This combination results in blocks that can be moulded easily into various shapes and sizes, adapting to different construction needs without compromising structural integrity.

From a cost perspective, these paving blocks are highly competitive. Because the primary raw material—plastic waste—is virtually free, production costs remain low. This allows communities to invest in infrastructure upgrades without the high expenses typically associated with paving stones. In many cases, the costs are comparable to traditional materials but with the added benefit of utilizing waste, reducing landfill and environmental pollution.

Beyond the technical and economic advantages, these paving solutions carry significant community value. They create visible, tangible improvements to shared spaces, elevating the quality of life and boosting local pride. Moreover, they are a perfect fit for "plastic-for-labour" programs, where community members earn wages or goods by collecting and processing plastic waste. This labour-backed model not only incentivizes cleanliness and recycling but also injects much-needed income into underserved areas.

In sum, plastic paving blocks and tiles are quiet champions of urban regeneration, turning discarded plastic into solid foundations for healthier, safer, and more vibrant communities.

Furniture and Fixtures

Upcycled plastic furniture and fixtures are emerging as practical, sustainable alternatives to traditional wood and metal pieces across a variety of settings worldwide. From grassroots DIY workshops and makerspaces to more organized recycling hubs, communities are crafting benches, school desks, shelves, and planter boxes from recycled plastic materials, creating durable, weatherproof solutions that stand the test of time.

What makes plastic furniture so appealing is the versatility and accessibility of the production process. Using extruded plastic lumber or pressed panels, makers can shape functional pieces with basic carpentry tools—no need for expensive machinery or industrial setups. This accessibility lowers the barrier to entry, enabling small groups and community projects to produce meaningful infrastructure on their own.

Functionality is key: these plastic creations are fully weatherproof, impervious to rot, splinters, and insect damage—problems that often plague wooden furniture, especially in outdoor or humid environments. This means furniture made from upcycled plastic can last many years longer with minimal maintenance, making it a sound investment even when upfront costs are similar to basic wood alternatives.

In terms of cost, plastic furniture often aligns with the price range of simple wooden pieces but offers superior longevity and resilience. Over time, these savings on replacement and repair add up, giving communities better value for their investment.

The community impact of these projects extends beyond cost and durability. Plastic furniture provides visible, tangible improvements in public spaces like parks, schools, and community centers. It's a quick win for local organizers and governments looking to enhance civic pride and beautify areas with sustainable materials. These items also serve as ideal branding or donation opportunities for nonprofits and businesses committed to social and environmental responsibility, building goodwill while promoting the circular economy.

In short, upcycled plastic furniture turns discarded materials into lasting assets that enrich communities both functionally and symbolically—furnishing spaces with strength, sustainability, and style born from waste.

Fencing and Drainage Channels

Upcycled plastic is proving to be a game-changer for essential infrastructure components like fencing and drainage systems, particularly in countries where budget constraints and environmental challenges make traditional materials expensive or impractical. In places like Nigeria, Pakistan, and Sri Lanka, communities are transforming plastic waste into robust perimeter fences and efficient drainage channels, addressing pressing needs while creating economic opportunities.

One of the biggest advantages of plastic fencing and drainage systems is their strength and durability. Unlike metal fences that can be stolen for scrap or wooden ones that rot and burn, plastic structures withstand harsh weather, pests, and vandalism, making them long-lasting and reliable. The inherent smoothness of plastic surfaces also prevents erosion and reduces blockages, a crucial feature for drainage channels that must maintain consistent water flow to prevent flooding and soil degradation.

Assembly is another highlight: plastic pieces can be joined using recycled plastic glue or simple heat-melting techniques, eliminating the need for complex tools or heavy machinery. This ease of construction enables small-scale workshops and microfactories to produce and install fencing and drainage solutions quickly and affordably.

Cost-wise, plastic fencing and drainage channels often come in at about one-third the price of equivalent cement or metal systems. This significant saving opens the door for widespread infrastructure improvements in low-income or underserved areas, where budgets for construction and maintenance are tight.

Beyond the physical infrastructure benefits, these products also carry tremendous community value. By converting plastic waste into useful construction materials, they help close critical infrastructure gaps, making neighbourhoods safer, more resilient, and better equipped to manage environmental risks like flooding. Moreover, the ongoing production and installation of these components fuel a growing ecosystem of local waste-to-income microfactories. These microfactories not only clean up communities but also create jobs and economic resilience, offering people a stable way to earn by transforming trash into treasure.

In essence, plastic fencing and drainage channels showcase how upcycling can deliver practical, cost-effective infrastructure that strengthens communities both physically and economically, building foundations for a cleaner, more sustainable future.

Everyday Utilities: Crates, Boxes, and Containers

Upcycling isn't limited to construction. Some of its most consistent wins come from replacing short-lived everyday items, especially in regions where cardboard and thin plastics degrade quickly or fail in wet climates. Enter the reusable crate, stackable box, and storage bin — essentials for markets, small businesses, warehouses, and households.

In countries like Mexico, Indonesia, and Ethiopia, plastic crates and containers made from shredded and remoulded waste are already being used to transport goods, store produce, and organize inventory in local shops. These products don't break down in the rain, don't attract termites or mould, and can last for years with minimal wear.

Take the example of the classic beer crate or beverage case — typically made of thick, impact-resistant plastic. These are ideal entry points for upcycling initiatives because the moulds are simple, the use-case is universal, and the durability is unmatched. Vendors and distributors love them because they stack well, protect glass, and don't warp under pressure.

Similarly, interlocking storage boxes or plastic baskets can be made from mixed plastic waste using extrusion or injection moulds. They become durable replacements for everything from cardboard moving boxes to woven baskets. And unlike cardboard, these upcycled versions don't disintegrate in humidity, making them perfect for tropical and rainy climates.

Cost Comparison

While the upfront production of a plastic crate may cost slightly more than a cardboard box, the lifecycle savings are enormous. A well-made plastic crate can be reused hundreds of times, whereas cardboard must be replaced after a single use, or immediately after a downpour. Over time, switching to plastic crates can cut packaging and transport costs by 30–50%, especially for small-scale vendors and cooperatives.

Community Value

These products empower small businesses, farmers, and informal vendors by giving them tools that last. They help reduce waste in packaging-heavy industries like agriculture, retail, and logistics, and they provide a steady output line for plastic microfactories to supply local markets with goods that are always in demand.

School and Office Supplies

Another promising frontier for upcycled plastic is in basic goods for schools and offices: clipboards, folders, storage bins, tabletops, and whiteboard frames. These products are flat, mouldable, and easy to produce in bulk. Countries like Ghana and Nepal have started producing low-cost school kits made from recycled plastic panels, durable enough to survive daily wear in rough environments.

By using locally sourced plastic waste, these kits drastically reduce the reliance on imported or short-lived goods, especially in rural schools where funding is minimal. It also makes educational access more sustainable. Kids aren't just showing up to cleaner schools, they're using tools made from the very waste their communities removed.

Product Ethics Policy for Community Upcycling Projects

Before you build anything from waste plastic, it's important to understand that not all plastics are safe for all uses, and not all uses are worth the risk.

This isn't about scaring people. It's about building credibility, keeping communities safe, and avoiding the kinds of mistakes that critics or regulators will use to shut good projects down.

Here are five key principles to guide what you should and shouldn't make:

Avoid Products That Come in Direct Human Contact

Especially when it involves:

- Babies and children

- Food and drink

- Skin or mouth contact

Plastics used in packaging, containers, or industrial applications often contain unknown additives, dyes, or residues. Some of these can leach harmful chemicals, especially when reheated, exposed to sunlight, or worn down through use.

Even if your plastic *looks* clean, there's no way to guarantee it's food-safe or toy-safe without expensive lab testing. Don't risk it.

Examples to avoid:

- Cups, plates, or bowls

- Baby toys or teething items

- Toothbrushes or personal hygiene products

- Reusable grocery bags that might carry food directly

Focus on Structural and Utility-Based Products

Upcycled plastic shines in strength, weather-resistance, and durability. So use it where those features matter — and where health risks are irrelevant.

Best use cases:

- Bricks, roofing tiles, and wall panels

- Public benches, planter boxes, and outdoor furniture

- Paving blocks, fencing, and drainage channels

- Storage crates, reusable bins, and construction forms

These products don't touch food or skin. They sit outdoors. They're not meant to be ingested or handled intimately. They're infrastructure, not household items.

Design for Durability, Not Disposability

Anything made from mixed waste plastic should be as permanent as possible. Products that will wear down quickly or be thrown away in a few months only create more microplastic pollution and defeat the purpose of upcycling.

Good upcycled products:

- Replace something you'd otherwise buy with concrete, wood, or metal

- Are designed to last 5–20 years (not five months)

- Can be reused, repaired, or remoulded

Think bricks, not bracelets.

Stay Ahead of Scrutiny

If you're doing this work in the open, or getting support from NGOs, donors, or local governments, people will eventually ask:
"Is this safe?"

Make it easy to answer:

- Avoid anything that would require medical or food-grade certification

- Be transparent about what plastics you're using and where they come from

- Stick to applications where risk is lowest and public benefit is highest

You don't need to meet international manufacturing codes, but you do need to show that you're being smart, careful, and responsible.

Remember: The Goal Is Trust

Upcycling is not just about materials, it's about momentum. You want people to believe in the value of this work.

One bad batch of unsafe products could set the movement back by years.

So lead with wisdom:

- Don't chase "cool" ideas if they come with health risks

- Don't sacrifice safety for speed

- Don't try to do it all; start with what works, prove it, then grow

Build things that last. Build things that matter.

And always build with the next community in mind.

Upcycling isn't about making art out of garbage. It's about reshaping economies — brick by brick, block by block. Every product made from plastic waste isn't just a recycled object. It's a proof of concept, a solution to a real problem, and a seed of a local economy that doesn't depend on imports, charity, or waiting for someone else to act.

Whether it's a plastic brick in Colombia, a wall panel in Kenya, or a roofing tile in Haiti, these builds tell a powerful story:
Plastic isn't waste. It's opportunity.

When designed ethically and used wisely, these products unlock something bigger than infrastructure. They restore dignity, create jobs, and give communities something most systems never gave them: ownership.

And because these designs are open-source and field-tested, they can spread fast — faster than the waste that inspired them.

So ask yourself:

- What does my community need most right now?

- What kind of plastic is piling up in the streets?

- What tools do we already have, or could build from scratch?

- What can we make that will *last* and prove the point?

Start small. Build one thing. Solve one problem. Then share it.

Because when people see what plastic can become — not in theory, but in practice — they believe.

And belief, like plastic, is remarkably durable.

This isn't just recycling.

This is rebuilding.

Why Recycling Failed and Upcycling Works

For decades, we've been told that tossing plastic into the blue bin was enough—that if we just sorted our waste correctly, the system would take care of the rest. It was a tidy solution to an ugly problem. The idea was comforting: you do your part, and the professionals will handle it from there. The messaging was clear and consistent—on packaging, in public service ads, even in schools. Recycle, and you're helping the planet.

But this narrative was more convenient than it was true. Especially when it came to plastic.

The reality is that traditional recycling, particularly plastic recycling, was never built to work at scale. It was a patchwork system rooted in good intentions, economic wishful thinking, and a heavy reliance on exporting the problem elsewhere. For years, wealthy countries shipped millions of tons of plastic waste to poorer nations under the label of "recyclables." But much of that plastic was contaminated, mixed, or low-value, and it ended up being burned, dumped, or mismanaged, causing more harm than good. Even domestically, most plastic that enters the recycling stream isn't truly recycled. It's sorted, stockpiled, or landfilled.

This failure wasn't just technical—it was systemic. The economics never added up. The process of cleaning, separating, and reprocessing plastic is energy-intensive and expensive, especially compared to producing new plastic from fossil fuels. Worse, many plastics degrade in quality each time they're recycled. So even when recycling happens, it often results in lower-grade, less useful products—a process known as *downcycling*. Over time, even the most recyclable plastics inch their way toward the dump.

Today, the truth is plain: the traditional model of plastic recycling is collapsing under its own weight. Global plastic production is still rising, while recycling rates remain stubbornly low. Public trust is eroding. And entire countries have banned imports of foreign plastic waste, forcing exporting nations to confront their inefficiencies.

Upcycling, by contrast, doesn't sell illusions. It delivers results.

Where recycling asked for trust, upcycling demands work. It's not a passive system built on invisible supply chains. It's a hands-on, community-based approach rooted in labour, design, and purpose.

Upcycling doesn't try to turn plastic back into what it was. Instead, it transforms plastic into what people need—roofing tiles, bricks, benches, walls, and walkways. It uses the material as-is, acknowledging its durability as a strength rather than a flaw. It doesn't hide the plastic. It puts it to work.

And because upcycling happens locally, it's grounded in context. The problems are visible, the solutions are tangible, and the value loop is closed right where the waste is generated. No overseas shipping. No wishful thinking. Just plastic, people, and purpose.

Upcycling isn't a feel-good story. It's a real-world strategy. A system of action for communities that can't afford to wait for global systems to fix themselves.

Where recycling offered a comfortable delusion, upcycling offers a hard-earned path forward—one built brick by brick, bottle by bottle, by the very people who were left out of the old solution.

The Blue Bin Lie

For years, the blue bin has symbolized environmental virtue. Drop your plastic in, and feel like you've done your part. But this symbol is built on a myth, because most of the plastic we put into those bins is never actually recycled.

Globally, only 9% of all plastic ever produced has been recycled. The rest has either been burned, buried, or left to pollute our landscapes and waterways. That number isn't a glitch — it's a structural failure.

Why? Because plastic recycling is far more complicated than it looks. For starters, plastic waste is rarely clean. It comes with food residue, labels, and dirt, which makes it difficult and expensive to sort. Then there's the variety of plastic types — not all plastics are created equal. Out of the seven commonly used categories, only Types 1 (PET) and 2 (HDPE) — like soda bottles and milk jugs — are widely accepted by recycling facilities. The rest? Films, bags, wrappers, multi-layered packaging? Straight to landfill or incineration.

Even when technically recyclable, many plastics degrade in quality during the process. That means fewer applications after recycling, and fewer companies willing to buy the end product.

For decades, much of the Western world's "recycled" plastic was simply shipped abroad to countries like China, Malaysia, or Indonesia. Out of sight, out of mind. But many of these countries lacked the infrastructure to handle the volume safely, so plastic was often burned in the open air or dumped in rivers and fields, with devastating environmental and human health impacts.

And then the loophole closed. In 2018, China banned the import of contaminated foreign waste. Others followed. Suddenly, the West had to confront its waste, and the cracks in the recycling story became impossible to ignore.

Even under ideal conditions, traditional plastic recycling requires immense energy, generates toxic byproducts, and leads to limited, low-value outputs. It was a system that looked good on paper and failed in practice. It made us feel responsible while offloading responsibility.

The blue bin wasn't a solution. It was a distraction.

Recycling Is Reverse Engineering

Traditional recycling treats plastic like it can be undone — like we can just wind back the clock and make it new again. But this is more wish than science. What's actually happening is reverse engineering: trying to unmake a complex, industrial product and rebuild it from the inside out.

That process is energy-intensive and technically demanding. Plastic has to be collected, cleaned, sorted, shredded, melted down, and sometimes chemically treated to isolate usable material. Every step adds cost. Every step adds emissions. And in the end, the return is modest — because most recycled plastic isn't as strong, as versatile, or as safe as the original.

Here's the catch: Plastic was never designed to be recycled indefinitely. Unlike glass or aluminum, which can loop through the system nearly forever, plastic degrades each time it's reprocessed. The polymers — long chains that give plastic its strength — get shorter and weaker with every cycle. This is why recycled plastic often becomes a lower-grade product: carpet fibres, filler material. It's called downcycling, and it's the rule, not the exception.

So while the recycling symbol implies a circle, the reality is a downward spiral — each turn bringing plastic closer to the landfill or the incinerator.

The system wasn't built for renewal. It was built for delay. And that delay comes at a massive financial and environmental cost.

Why Upcycling Works

Upcycling flips the script on plastic waste.

Instead of trying to erase the material's past — melting it down, separating molecules, stripping it of its flaws — upcycling accepts plastic for what it already is: a tough, durable, waterproof, and mouldable resource. It doesn't try to turn plastic back into plastic bottles or food packaging. It turns it into something *new*—something *useful-with* as little fuss (and fuel) as possible.

That shift in mindset makes all the difference. Here's why:

➤ Lower Energy Use
Where traditional recycling relies on high-temperature industrial processes, upcycling uses basic tools: heat, pressure, and simple moulds. A community-powered machine can turn shredded plastic into bricks or panels using the energy of a hotplate and a hand press, or even solar heat. This slashes the energy footprint and cuts out the need for specialized infrastructure.

➤ Decentralized and Local
Upcycling works best in small, distributed workshops. Whether it's a garage, a converted shipping container, or a schoolyard co-op, people can build what they need with local waste and local labour. No trucks hauling trash across borders. No middlemen. Just communities reclaiming their materials and reshaping their environment.

➤ Works with "Unrecyclables"
Food wrappers. Laminated bags. Mixed plastic streams. The stuff no recycling plant wants. Upcycling welcomes them. These difficult materials

are perfect for making rugged goods — like wall panels, fence posts, or roofing tiles — where beauty and purity matter less than durability and cost.

➤ Durable, Long-Lasting Results
This isn't craft-day repurposing. Upcycled products can be stronger and longer-lasting than the materials they replace. Plastic bricks resist rot, mould, termites, and water. Tiles made from trash can survive tropical storms. Benches made from extruded plastic lumber don't splinter, rust, or need repainting. It's not decoration — it's infrastructure.

In short, upcycling doesn't pretend plastic can be reborn. It gives it a second life with an honest purpose and functional value. Where recycling chases purity, upcycling chases *possibility* — and gets results the first time around.

Cost and Outcome Comparison

Metric	Traditional Recycling	Upcycling
Energy use	High (melting, separating)	Low to moderate (heating, moulding)

Infrastructure	Centralized, expensive	Decentralized, accessible
Output quality	Downgraded plastic	Functional, durable goods
Waste acceptance	Strictly limited	Broad, includes "unrecyclables"
Environmental impact	Often invisible but significant	Tangible, local, and visible
Economic model	Global, fragile, profit-driven	Local, circular, community-based

Upcycling Is Proof, Not a Promise

Traditional recycling systems rely on a kind of public faith: throw your plastic in the blue bin, and *somewhere, someone* will deal with it. It's a promise made by cities, corporations, and policymakers —

often without the infrastructure or accountability to back it up.

Upcycling doesn't ask for your belief. It hands you a brick, a bench, a roof. Tangible outcomes, built from yesterday's trash, made by the same hands that once struggled to throw it away. No abstractions. No delays. Just direct transformation.

And because upcycling happens locally, it puts agency where it belongs — in the hands of communities. It's not waiting for national waste policy to shift or for international plastic treaties to be signed. It's working now, block by block, kilo by kilo.

Unlike recycling's centralized, expensive, and often invisible process, upcycling operates in plain sight. In garages, microfactories, community centres — wherever there's waste, need, and someone willing to build.

It doesn't need billion-dollar plants or perfect sorting systems. It needs basic tools, willing hands, and a clear mission:
Turn waste into worth. Right here. Right now.

The Real Test: Outcomes

At its core, the difference between recycling and upcycling comes down to intent and impact.

Traditional recycling is driven by market demand. It asks, *"How do we process this waste into something that can be sold back into the system?"* The goal is resale. Commodity. Profit. That's why it depends so heavily on purity, scale, and energy-intensive infrastructure, because the outcome must fit within an economic model built for big players and global trade.

Upcycling flips the question. It asks, *"What do people around me need?"*

It's not about making plastic disappear — it's about making it matter. A plastic bottle doesn't become another cheap bottle. It becomes a brick that forms a classroom. A tile that shields a family from the rain. A bench that creates a public gathering space.

These aren't speculative outputs. They don't sit in limbo, waiting for buyers or subsidies. They go straight into solving real problems: housing shortages, poor infrastructure, unemployment, and pollution.

The value isn't theoretical. It's lived.

Where recycling often delays the inevitable — a trip to the landfill, just a few years later — upcycling gives plastic a second life with purpose. One that's durable, visible, and needed.

Because when waste is turned into something useful, not just *sellable*, it becomes more than material. It becomes proof that we don't need to wait for the system to save us.

We can build the solution ourselves.

Recycling failed not because people didn't care, but because the system didn't. It was a feel-good ritual built on flawed logistics, overseas dependence, and an unrealistic belief that all plastic could be reborn endlessly. In reality, it exported the burden and disguised the breakdown.

Upcycling works because it flips that script. It stays local. It makes results visible. And it invites people not to "dispose" but to *build*. It turns waste into work, plastic into product, and despair into direction.

Where recycling asked for trust in a broken system, upcycling asks for effort — and gives back proof.

It's not just about reusing plastic.

It's about reclaiming *agency*.

That's the real product. And that's a promise worth keeping.

Last Word

If there is a single message that carries through every chapter of this book, it's this: you don't need a revolution to begin. You just need a build.

For decades, the world has been sold the idea that massive, centralized systems would solve the plastic crisis — that if we just placed our bottles in the right bins, someone, somewhere, would take care of the rest. But the system was never really designed to work. Recycling outsourced responsibility, prioritized profit over people, and relied on global chains that were invisible, fragile, and unaccountable. It asked for faith without proof.

Upcycling, by contrast, doesn't ask for belief. It delivers results. It turns a bottle into a brick. A wrapper into a wall. A pile of trash into a place to sit, to gather, to build. The results are local, physical, and immediately useful — not theoretical, not deferred, and not outsourced.

When you create something that your community can see and use, you don't just reduce waste — you raise standards. You don't just clean a space — you invite dignity back into it. The transformation isn't just of the plastic. It's of the people. The psychology. The sense of power and ownership that starts to take root when someone realizes, *"I did that. We did that."*

A Thousand Possibilities Begin with One

The question isn't whether the world can be changed by plastic upcycling. The question is who will go first. Because what one person builds, others can replicate. What one neighbourhood does, another can adopt. When a bench made of waste appears in a schoolyard, it tells the next village: You can do this, too. And when that story spreads, the impact multiplies.

You don't need permission from governments or corporations. You don't need millions in funding or access to cutting-edge technology. You need:

- The problem in plain sight

- The plastic already piling up

- A mould, a shredder, or even a makeshift press

- And a community ready to build something better

From that modest foundation, closed-loop economies can emerge — not as abstract theory, but as *visible infrastructure*: bricks, blocks, benches, tiles, walls, walkways. Each product proving that value doesn't have to be extracted from the earth. It can be recovered from what the world tried to throw away.

Not Clean. Not Perfect. But Ours.

Let's be honest: upcycling isn't easy. It's not glamorous. It's messy, labour-intensive, and often slow. But it's real. It's honest. And it works. It doesn't create greenwashed illusions of sustainability — it creates shelter. Jobs. Safer streets. Stronger homes. It turns trash into trust.

The truth is, no one's coming to save us with perfect solutions. But we can save each other with imperfect ones — starting right where we are, with what we already have.

So before you wait for someone else to fix it, ask yourself:

- What does your community need most right now — shelter, seating, pathways, protection?

- What kind of plastic waste do you see every day?

- What's the simplest, scrappiest thing you can build that solves a real problem?

Build that. Document it. Share it.

Not because you want applause, but because someone, somewhere, is also surrounded by waste and wondering where to begin. Let your success be their shortcut. Let your brick be their blueprint.

This Isn't a Movement. It's a Method.

Revolutions don't start with slogans. They start with *examples*. And a single, working build — in a village, an alley, a schoolyard — can ignite a ripple effect that reaches farther than the plastic itself ever could.

Because in the end, this work is not about plastic. It's about *agency* — reclaiming the right to build value where the system saw only waste. It's about telling a new story with every product made:

"This didn't come from a factory.
 This came from us."

You're not just upcycling plastic.

You're upcycling participation.

Upcycling pride.

Upcycling purpose.

And that's the kind of economy worth fighting for.

So here's your invitation:

Pick one project.

Build one thing.

And let that one thing lead to everything.

THE END

www.ingramcontent.com/pod-product-compliance
Lightning Source LLC
Chambersburg PA
CBHW062132020426
42335CB00013B/1192